A.S.A.P. ABSTRACTS PUBLISHING

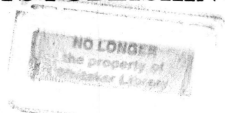

PROFESSIONAL EDUCATOR

CONTENT AND FULL EXAM
Florida Teacher Certification Exam

Written By:

Dr. Ron Dawson PHD Psychology/school drop out prevention
Carol Dettling BS Elementary
Ann Guest MS English , Miami School Board
Dr. Jerry Holt PHD Science
Debbie McCray MS School Administration
Dennis McCray Licensed Clinical Social Worker
Sue Nadler MS English
Marlyn Rainear MS Library Science
Kathy Schnirman M. Ed Emotionally Handicapped
Fran Thew MS Computer Science
Betty Turso MS English

Printed in the United States of America

Praxis II Principles of Learning and Teaching
ISBN: 1-58197-004-8

TABLE OF CONTENTS

1. 0   Applies knowledge of physical, social, and academic developmental patterns and of individual differences, to meet the instructional needs of all students in the classroom and to advise students about those needs.

2.0   Enhances students' feelings of dignity and self-worth and the worth of other people including those from other ethnic, cultural, linguistic and economic groups.

3.0   Arranges and manages the physical environment to facilitate instruction and ensure student safety

4.0   Recognizes overt signs of severe emotional distress in students and demonstrates awareness of appropriate intervention and referral procedures

5.0   Recognizes signs of alcohol and drug abuse in students and demonstrates awareness of appropriate intervention and referral procedures.

6.0   Recognizes the overt physical and behavioral indicators of child abuse and neglect, knows the rights and responsibilities regarding reporting and how to interact appropriately with a child after a report has been made.

7.0   Examine and apply copyright laws appropriately.

8.0   Deals with misconduct, interruptions, intrusions, and digressions in ways that promote instructional momentum.

9.0   Determines the entry level knowledge and/or skills of students for a given set of instructional objectives using diagnostic tests, teacher observations, and student records.

10.0   Identify long-range goals for a given subject area

11.0   Constructs and sequences related short -range goals for a given subject area.

12.0 Selects, adapts, and/or develops instructional materials for a given set of instructional objectives and student learning needs

13.0 Selects/develops and sequences learning activities that are appropriate to instructional objectives and students needs.

14.0 Uses class time efficiently.

15.0 Communicates effectively using verbal and non-verbal skills

16.0 Creates and maintains academic focus by using verbal, nonverbal and/or visual or motivational devices.

17.0 Presents forms of knowledge such as concepts, laws and law-like principles, academic rules, and value knowledge.

18.0 Presents directions appropriate for carrying out an instructional activity.

19.0 Stimulates and directs student thinking, and checks student comprehension through appropriate questioning techniques.

20.0 Provides appropriate practice to promote learning and retention.

21.0 Relates to students' verbal communications in ways that encourage participations and maintains academic focus.

22.0 Uses feedback procedures that give information of students about the appropriateness of their response (s).

23.0 Conducts reviews of subject matter.

24.0 Constructs or assembles classroom tests and tasks to measure student achievement of objectives.

25.0 Establishes a testing environment in which students can validly demonstrate their knowledge and/or skill, and receive adequate information about the quality of their test performance

26.0 Utilizes an effective system for maintaining records of student and class progress.

27.0 Uses computers in education.

COMPETENCY/Skill

COMPETENCY 1.0   **Applies knowledge of physical, social, and academic developmental patterns and of individual differences, to meet the instructional needs of all students in the classroom and to advise students about those needs.**

Skill 1.1 Recognizes patterns of physical, social, and academic development of students in the classroom including those with exceptionalities.

The teacher has a broad knowledge and thorough understanding of the development that typically occurs during the students' current period of life. More importantly, the teacher understands how children learn best during each period of development. The most important premise of child development is that all domains of development (physical, social, and academic) are integrated. Development in each dimension is influenced by the other dimensions. Moreover, today's educator must also have a knowledge of exceptionalities and how these exceptionalities effect all domains of a child's development.

Physical Development

It is important for the teacher to be aware of the physical stage of development and how the child's physical growth and development effect the child's learning. Factors determined by the physical stage of development include: ability to sit and attend, the need or activity, the relationship between physical skills and self-esteem, and the degree to which physical involvement in an activity (as opposed to being able to understand an abstract concept) effects learning.

Cognitive (Academic) Development

Children go through patterns of learning beginning with preoperational thought processes and moving to concrete operational thoughts. Eventually they begin to acquire the mental ability to think about and solve problems in their head because they can manipulate objects symbolically. Children of most ages can use symbols such as words and numbers to represent objects and relations, but they need concrete reference points. It is essential that children be encouraged to use and develop the thinking skills that they possess in solving problems that interest them. The content of the curriculum must be relevant, engaging, and meaningful to the students.

Social Development

Children progress through a variety of social stages beginning with an awareness of peers but a lack of concern for their presence. Young children engage in "parallel" activities playing alongside their peers without directly interacting with one another. During the primary years, children develop an intense interest in peers. They establish productive, positive social and working relationships with one another. This stage of social growth continues to increase in importance throughout the child's school years including intermediate, middle school, and high school years. It is necessary for the teacher to recognize the importance of developing positive peer group relationships and to provide opportunities and support for cooperative small group projects that not only develop cognitive ability but promote peer interaction. The ability to work and relate effectively with peers is of major importance and contributes greatly to the child's sense of competence. In order to develop this sense of competence, children need to be successful at acquiring the knowledge and skills recognized by our culture as important, especially those skills which promote academic achievement.

Knowledge of age-appropriate expectations is fundamental to the teacher's positive relationship with students and effective instructional strategies. Equally important is the knowledge of what is individually appropriate for the specific children in a classroom. Developmentally-oriented teachers approach classroom groups and individual students with a respect for their emerging capabilities. Developmentists recognize that kids grow in common patterns, but at different rates which usually cannot be speeded up by adult pressure or input. Developmentally-oriented teachers know that variance in the school performance of different children often results from differences in their general growth. With the establishment of inclusionary classes throughout the schools, it is vital for all teachers to know the characteristics of students' exceptionalities and their implications on learning.

Skill 1.2 Obtains knowledge of students through tests, observations, and student records and interprets the information to students, parents and other appropriate personnel.

The teacher appreciates the importance of knowing and understanding students in order to provide the most effective learning opportunities. Therefore the teacher is aware of and uses a variety of strategies for developing this knowledge of students' strengths and weaknesses and is able to share this knowledge with the students, their parents, and others.

It is of significant importance to remember that the main purpose of evaluation in education is to guide instruction. Therefore tests must measure not only what a child has learned, but also what a child has yet to learn and what a teacher must teach. Although

FLORIDA TEACHER CERTIFICATION EXAM

today's educator utilizes many forms of assessment, testing remains an integral part of instruction and evaluation.

Tests are essential for the learner in understanding his/her capacities, achievement, and learning difficulties. Because of the influence tests can have upon students, they should not be taken lightly, nor should they be given haphazardly. In order for a test to be an accurate measurement of student progress, the teacher must know how to plan and construct tests. No longer can a teacher rely on "ready made" tests to precisely assess what students know. In addition, the teacher must know how to administer tests, how to prepare students in the knowledge and skills of test-taking, and how to provide feedback on test performance. Research indicates that students do their best when they are both motivated and aware of and able to apply test-taking skills. It is therefore important that teachers first motivate students to put forth their best efforts and that they prepare them in test-taking skills.

The ways that a teacher uses test data is a meaningful aspect of instruction and may increase the motivation level of the students especially when this information is available in the form of feedback to the students. This feedback should indicate to the students what they need to do in order to improve their achievement. Frequent testing and feedback is most often an effective way to increase achievement.

Standardized testing is currently under great scrutiny but educators agree that any test that serves as a means of gathering and interpreting information about children's learning and which can provide accurate, helpful input for nurturing children's further growth, is acceptable. All testing must be formative in nature. Formative evaluation is the basic, everyday kind of assessment which teachers continually do to understand students' growth and to help them learn further.

Observations

Valuable information can be obtained through teacher observations. Teachers are constantly observing students and making assessments about their performance that in turn influence future instruction. Informal observations allow teachers to observe students with no predetermined focus. Through such observations teachers may become aware of students in their classes who are able to work independently or who may require a great deal of guidance. Informal assessments provide important information and are frequently the basis for parent conferences.

A "global observation" is a teacher's written account of a student's interaction with peers, a student's general attitude towards school and learning, the student's overall ability to satisfactorily complete assignments, and the student's typical behavior. A "global observation" is written in lay terms without educational jargon and is therefore easily understood by parents. Because it contains pertinent information about a child's class performance, it is a valuable tool for school administrators, guidance counselors, psychologists, and other personnel who may be involved with the child.

A "behavioral observation" is a written anecdotal record of a child's behavior and activities for a specific period of time. The teacher records both the beginning and ending times for the observation and precisely indicates the child's every movement, utterance, and action during that designated time. This type of observation is valuable in determining a child's activity level and ability to attend.

Occasionally more formal observations are needed. Formal observations have a specified focus and sample behavior to be observed systematically. Some goals or objectives can only be assessed by observation such as those that occur during cooperative group activities. Formal observations often allow teachers to profit from new information that may challenge some of their opinions about students. Student records consist of a history of a child's education. Meaningful information such as the child's attendance, grade averages, and general health are described. Some basic information about the child's family, current address and schools attended is included. Standardized test scores and dates of administration are also an important aspect of the student's record.

The narrative is a written record which may be contained within a student's cumulative record. Teachers can use this information to set goals for individual students or to structure future activities. The information acquired through any of these tools can best be reported through a parent/student conference or a meeting with other educators. Although written reports can be devised that could summarize the details and data of the knowledge which the teacher has gained, a more thorough explanation can be presented through a face to face meeting.

Skill 1.3 Demonstrates a knowledge of motivational factors or conditions which encourage students to be achievement oriented and goal directed.

Teachers need to be aware that much of what they say and do can be motivating and may have a positive effect on students' achievement. Studies have been conducted to determine the impact of teacher behavior on student performance. Surprisingly, a teacher's voice can really make an impression on students. Teachers' voices have several dimensions - volume, pitch, rate, etc. A recent study on the effects of speech rate indicates that, although both boys and girls prefer to listen at the rate of about 200 words per minute, boys tend to prefer slower rates overall than girls. This same study indicates that a slower rate of speech directly effects processing ability and comprehension.

Other speech factors such as communication of ideas, communication of emotion, distinctness/pronunciation, quality variation and phrasing correlate with teaching criterion scores. These scores show that "good" teachers ("good" meaning teachers who positively impact and motivate students) use more variety in speech than do "less effective" teachers. A teacher's speech skills can be strong motivating elements. A teacher's body language has an even greater effect on student achievement and ability to set and focus on goals. Teacher smiles provide support and give feedback about the teacher's affective state. A deadpan expression can actually be a detriment to the student's progress. Teacher frowns are perceived by students to mean displeasure, disapproval, and even anger. Studies also show that teacher posture and movement are indicators of the teacher's enthusiasm and energy which emphatically influence student learning, attitudes, motivation, and focus on goals. Teachers have a greater efficacy on student motivation than any person other than parents.

Teachers can also enhance student motivation by planning and directing interactive, "hands-on" learning experiences. Research substantiates that cooperative group projects decrease student behavior problems and increase student on-task behavior. Students who are directly involved with learning activities are more motivated to complete a task to the best of their ability.

Skill 1.4 Demonstrates knowledge of school and community resources for students who have special needs.

A teacher's responsibility to students extends beyond the four walls of the school building. In addition to offering well-planned and articulately delivered lessons, the teacher must consider the effects of both body language and spoken language on students' learning. Furthermore, today's educator must address the needs of diverse learners within a single classroom. The teacher is able to attain materials that may be necessary for the majority of the regular education students and some of the special needs children and, more and more frequently, one individual student. The "effective" teacher knows that there are currently hundreds of adaptive materials which could be used to help these students increase achievement and develop skills.

Student-centered classrooms contain not only textbooks, workbooks, and literature materials but also rely heavily on a variety of audio-visual equipment and computers. There are tape recorders, language masters, filmstrip projectors, and laser disc players to help meet the learning styles of the students.

Although most school centers cannot supply all the materials that special needs students require, each district more than likely has a resource center where teachers can check out special equipment. Most communities support agencies which offer assistance in providing the necessities of special needs people including students. Teachers must know how to obtain a wide range of materials including school supplies, medical care, clothing, food, adaptive computers and books (such as Braille), eye glasses, hearing aids, wheelchairs, counseling, transportation, etc.

A teacher's job would be relatively easy if simply instructing students in current curriculum objectives was his/her primary responsibility. Today's educator must first assure that the students are able to come to school, are able to attend to the curriculum, have individual learning styles met, and are motivated to work to their fullest capacity.

Most special needs students have an Individual Educational Plan or a 504 Plan. These documents clearly state the students' educational objectives and learning needs as well as persons responsible for meeting these objectives. A well-written Individual Educational Plan will contain evidence that the student is receiving resources from the school and the community which will assist in meeting the physical, social and academic needs of the student.

The challenges of meeting the needs of all students in the classroom require that the teacher be a lifelong learner. Ongoing participation in professional staff development, attendance at local, state, and national conferences, and continuing education classes help teachers grow in many ways including in an awareness of resources available for students.

Skill 1.5 Matches learner needs with instructional elements.

If an educational program is child-centered, then it will surely address the abilities and needs of the students because it will take its cues from students' interests, concerns, and questions. Making an educational program child-centered involves building on the natural curiosity children bring to school, and asking children what they want to learn.

Teachers help students to identify their own questions, puzzles, and goals, and then structure for them widening circles of experience and investigation of those topics. Teachers manage to infuse all the skills, knowledge, and concepts that society mandates into a child-driven curriculum. This does not mean passive teachers who respond only to students' explicit cues. Teachers also draw on their understanding of children's developmentally characteristic needs and enthusiasms to design experiences that lead children into areas they might not choose, but that they do enjoy and that engage them. Teachers also bring their own interests and enthusiasms into the classroom to share and to act as a motivational means of guiding children.

Implementing such a child-centered curriculum is the result of very careful and deliberate planning. Planning serves as a means of organizing instruction and influences classroom teaching. Well thought-out planning includes specifying behavioral objectives, specifying students' entry behavior (knowledge and skills), selecting and sequencing learning activities so as to move students from entry behavior to objective, and evaluating the outcomes of instruction in order to improve planning.

Planning for instructional activities entails identification or selection of the activities which the teacher and students will engage in during a period of instruction. Planning is a multifaceted activity which includes the following considerations: the determination of the order in which activities will be completed; the specification of the component parts of an activity, including their order; the materials to be used for each part, and the particular roles of the teacher and students; decisions about the amount of time to be spent on a given activity and the number of activities to be completed during a period of instruction; judgment of the appropriateness of an activity for a particular situation; and specifications of the organization of the class for the activity.

Attention to learner needs during planning is foremost and includes identification of

FLORIDA TEACHER CERTIFICATION EXAM

that which the students already know or need to know; the matching of learner needs with instructional elements such as content, materials, activities, and goals; and the determination of whether or not students have performed at an acceptable level, following instruction.

COMPETENCY 2.0   Enhances students' feelings of dignity and self-worth and the worth of other people including those from other ethnic, cultural , linguistic and economic groups.

Skill 2.1   Demonstrates instructional and inter-personal skills which assist students in developing a positive self-concept.

A positive self-concept for a child or adolescent is a very important element in terms of the students' ability to learn and to be an integral member of society. If students think poorly of themselves or have sustained feelings of inferiority, they probably will not be able to optimize their potentials for learning. It is therefore part of the teacher's task to ensure that each student develops a positive self-concept.

A positive self concept does not imply feelings of superiority, perfection, or competence/efficacy.   Instead, a positive self-concept involves self-acceptance as a person, liking himself or herself, and having a proper respect for oneself. The teacher who encourages these factors has contributed to the development of a positive self-concept in students.

Teachers may take a number of approaches to enhancement of self-concept among students. One such scheme is the process approach, which proposes a three-phase model for teaching. This model includes a sensing function, a transforming function, and an acting function. These three factors can be simplified into the words by which the model is usually given: reach, touch, and teach. The sensing, or perceptual, function, incorporates information or stimuli in an intuitive manner. The transforming function conceptualizes, abstracts, evaluates, and provides meaning and value to perceived information.   The acting function chooses actions from several different alternatives to be set forth overtly. The process model may be applied to almost any curricular field.

An approach which aims directly at the enhancement of self concept is designated Invitational Education. According to this approach, teachers and their behaviors may be inviting or they may be disinviting.   Inviting behaviors enhance self-concept among students, while disinviting behaviors diminish self-concept.

Disinviting behaviors include those which demean students, as well as those which may be chauvinistic, sexist, condescending, thoughtless, or insensitive to student feelings. Inviting behaviors are the opposite of these, and characterize teachers who act with consistency and sensitivity.   Inviting teacher behaviors reflect an attitude of "doing with" rather than "doing to." Students are "invited" or "disinvited" depending on the teacher behaviors.

Invitational teachers exhibit the following skills(Biehler and Snowman, 394):

1. Reaching each student (e.g., learning names, having one-to-one contact)
2. Listening with care (e.g., picking up subtle cues)
3. Being real with students(e.g., providing only realistic praise, "coming on straight")
4. Being real with oneself (e.g., honestly appraising your own feelings and disappointments)
5. Inviting good discipline (e.g., showing students you have respect in personal ways)
6. Handling rejection (e.g., not taking lack of student response in personal ways)
7. Inviting oneself (e.g., thinking positively about oneself)

Skill 2.2 Demonstrates instructional and inter-personal skills which assist students in interacting constructively with their peers.

Cooperative learning situations, as practiced in today's classrooms, grew out of search conducted by several groups in the early 1970's. Cooperative learning situations can range from very formal applications such as STAD (Student Teams-Achievement Divisions) and CIRC (Cooperative Integrated Reading and Composition) to less formal groupings known variously as "group investigation," "learning together", "discovery groups". Cooperative learning as a general term is now firmly recognized and established as a teaching and learning technique in American schools.

Since cooperative learning techniques are so widely diffused in the schools, it is necessary to orient students in the skills by which cooperative learning groups can operate smoothly, and thereby enhance learning. Students who cannot interact constructively with other students will not be able to take advantage of the learning opportunities provided by the cooperative learning situations and will furthermore deprive their fellow students of the opportunity for cooperative learning.

The skills that form the hierarchy of cooperation in which students first learn to work together as a group, then proceed to levels at which they may engage in simulated conflict situations, so that different points of view may be constructively entertained.

Further, the theorists provided a list of strategies for the teacher in teaching cooperative skills (Johnson, Johnson, Holubec, and Roy, 1984):

To teach cooperative skills, the teacher should:

1. Ensure that students see the need for the skill.
2. Ensure that students understand what the skill is and when it should be used.

3. Set up practice situations and encourage mastery of the skill.
4. Ensure that students have the time and the needed procedures for discussing (and receiving feedback on)how well they are using the skill.

5. Ensure that students persevere in practicing the skill until the skill seems a natural action.

A further goal of cooperative learning techniques is to establish and/or enhance mutual respect for other students. Cooperative learning can promote positive social goals when used effectively as a teaching /learning tool. When the teacher promotes interaction of students among ethnic and/or social goals when used effectively as a teaching tool. When the teacher promotes interaction of students among ethnic and/or social groups, students tend to respond positively by forming friendships and having enhanced respect for other sociological groups. Thus, the teacher who effectively manages cooperative learning groups has not only promoted cognitive learning, but has also promote desirable behaviors in terms of mutual respect for all students.

COMPETENCY 3.0   Identifies physical elements and arrangements in the classroom that directly affect learning and/or safety.

The physical setting of the classroom contributes a great deal toward the propensity for students to learn. An adequate, well-built, and well-equipped classroom will invite students to learn. This has been called "invitational learning".

Among the important factors to consider in the physical setting of the

classroom are the following:
1. adequate physical space
2. repair status
3. lighting adequacy
4. adequate entry/exit access (including handicap accessibility)
5. ventilation/climate control
6. coloration

A classroom must have adequate physical space so that students can conduct themselves comfortably. Some students are distracted by windows, pencil sharpeners, doors, etc. Some students prefer the front, middle or back rows.

The teacher has the responsibility to report any items of classroom disrepair to maintenance staff. Broken windows, falling plaster, exposed sharp surfaces, leaks in ceiling or walls, and other items of disrepair present hazards to students.

Another factor which must be considered is adequate lighting. Report any inadequacies in classroom illumination. Florescent lights placed at acute angles often burn out faster. A healthy supply of spare tubes is a sound investment.

Local fire and safety codes dictate entry and exit standards. In addition, all corridors and classrooms should be wheelchair accessible for students and others who use them. Older schools may not have this accessibility.

Another consideration is adequate ventilation and climate control. Florida classrooms use air conditioning extensively. Sometimes it is so cold as to be considered a distraction. Specialty classes such as science require specialized hoods for ventilation. Physical Education classes have the added responsibility for shower areas and specialized environments that must be heated such as pool or athletic training rooms.

Classrooms with warmer subdued colors contribute to students' concentration on task items. Neutral hues for coloration of walls, ceiling, and carpet or tile are generally used in classrooms so that distraction due to classroom coloration may be minimized.

Skill 3.2 Arranges classroom furniture, equipment, and instructional aids to facilitate teaching, learning, and safety.

In the modern classroom, there is a great deal of furniture, equipment, supplies, appliances, and learning aids to help the teacher teach and students learn. The classroom should be provided with furnishing which fit the purpose of the classroom. The kindergarten classroom may have a reading center, a playhouse, a puzzle table, student work desks/tables, a sandbox, and any other relevant learning/interest areas.

Whatever the arrangement of furniture and equipment may be the teacher must provide for adequate traffic flow. Rows of desks must have adequate space between them for students to move and for the teacher to circulate. All areas must be open to line-of-sight supervision by the teacher.

In all cases, proper care must be taken to ensure student safety. Furniture and equipment should be situated safely at all times. No equipment, materials, boxes, etc. should be placed where there is danger of falling over. Doors must have entry and exit accessibility at all times.

Skill 3.3 Organizes an effective system for placement and distribution of materials in the classroom.

Instructional momentum requires an organized system for material placement and distribution. Inability to find an overhead transparency, a necessary chart page, or the handout worksheet for the day not only stops the momentum, but is very irritating to students. Materials not appearing in an expected classroom site frustrates both teacher and students. Major categories on the Florida Performance Measurement System instrument are "Handles materials well" and "Maintains instructional momentum."

In the lower grades an organized system uses a "classroom helper" for effective distribution and collection of books, equipment, supplies, etc. The classroom helpers should be taught to replace the materials in the proper places to obtain them easily for the next time they are used. Periodically, the teacher should inspect to see that all materials are in the proper places and are ready for use as needed.

At higher grade levels, the teacher is concerned with materials such as textbooks, written instructional aids, worksheets, computer programs, etc. which must be produced, maintained, distributed, and collected for future use. One important consideration is the production of sufficient copies of duplicated materials to satisfy classroom needs. Another is the efficient distribution of worksheets and other materials. The teacher may decide to hand out materials as students are in their learning sites (desks, etc.), or to have distribution materials at a clearly specified place (or small number of places) in the classroom. In any case, there should be firmly established procedures, completely understood by student for receiving classroom materials. Special fields such as physical education or media specialists are well schooled in these areas.

Skill 3.4   Identifies appropriate procedures for movement of students in emergencies that can be anticipated.

Statutes state only the following with regard to school emergencies:
235.14 Emergency drills. - The Department of Education shall formulate and prescribe rules and instructions for emergency drills for all the public schools of the state which comprise grades K-12 and for the School for the Deaf and the Blind. Each administrator or teacher in charge of such a facility shall be provided a   copy of the rules and instructions; and each such person shall see that such emergency drills are held at least once each calendar quarter and that all personnel and students are properly instructed regarding such rules and instructions.

This statute addresses only instructions for drills, not for actual emergency procedures. Among the possible emergencies that have been identified which schools might face are fire, flood, tornado, bomb threat, chemical accident, traffic related chemical spills (i.e. Boynton Beach, Fl. 1996), earthquake and hurricanes. The primary concern in emergency situations is the physical safety and well-being of students. The teacher must be thoroughly familiar with the prescribed movement of students in emergency situations in order to minimize danger to the students and to other school personnel.

The major emergency responses include two categories for student movement: tornado warning response; and building evacuation, which includes most other emergencies (fire, bomb threat, etc.). For tornadoes, the prescribed response is to evacuate all students and personnel to the first floor of multi-story buildings, and to place students along walls away from windows. All persons, including the teacher, should then crouch on the floor and cover their heads with their hands. These are standard procedures for severe weather, particularly tornadoes.

Most other emergency situations require evacuation of the school building. Teachers should be thoroughly familiar with evacuation routes established for each classroom in which he or she teaches. The teacher should accompany and supervise students throughout the evacuation procedure, and check to see that all students under his or her supervision are accounted for. The teacher should then continue to supervise students until the building may be reoccupied (upon proper school or community authority), or until other procedures are followed for students to officially leave the school area and cease to be the supervisory responsibility of the school. Elementary students evacuated to another school can wear name tags and parents or guardians should sign them out at a central location.

COMPETENCY 4.0 Recognizes overt signs of severe emotional distress in students and demonstrates awareness of appropriate intervention and referral procedures.

Skill 4.1 Knows and can distinguish between typical behavior and severe emotional distress in students.

All students demonstrate some behaviors that may indicate emotional distress from time to time since all children experience stressful periods within their lives. However, the emotionally healthy student can maintain control of their own behavior even during stressful times. Teachers need to be mindful that the difference between typical stressful behavior and severe emotional distress is determined by the frequency, duration, and intensity of stressful behavior.

Lying, stealing, and fighting are atypical behaviors that most children may exhibit occasionally, but if a child lies, steals, or fights regularly or blatantly, then these behaviors may be indicative of emotional distress. Lying is especially common among young children who feel the need to avoid punishment or as a means to make themselves feel more important. As children become older, past the ages of six or seven, lying is often a signal that the child is feeling insecure. These feelings of insecurity may escalate to the point of being habitual or obvious and then may indicate that the child is seeking attention because of emotional distress. Fighting, especially among siblings, is a common occurrence. However, if a child fights, is unduly aggressive, or is belligerent towards others on a long-term basis, teachers and parents need to consider the possibility of emotional problems.

How can a teacher know when a child needs help with his/her behavior? The child will indicate by what they do that they need and want help. Breaking rules established by parents, teachers, and other authorities and destroying property can signify that a student is losing control especially when these behaviors occur frequently. Other signs that a child needs help may include frequent bouts of crying, a quarrelsome attitude, constant complaints about school, friends, or life in general. Anytime a child's disposition, attitude, or habits change significantly, teachers and parents need to seriously consider the existence of emotional difficulties.

Emotional disturbances in childhood are not uncommon and take a variety of forms. Usually these problems show up in the form of uncharacteristic behaviors. Most of the time, children respond favorably to brief treatment programs of psychotherapy. At other times, disturbances may need more intensive therapy and are harder to resolve. All stressful behaviors need to be addressed and any type of chronic antisocial behavior needs to be examined as a possible symptom of deep-seated emotional upset.

Skill 4.2 Recognizes overt indicators of severe emotional stress, including behaviors typical of those who attempt suicide.

Neurotic Disorders

Sometimes emotional disorders escalate so severely that the child's well-being is threatened. Teachers and parents must recognize the signs of severe emotional stress which may become detrimental to the child. There are various forms of emotional disorders which can be potentially dangerous including neurotic disorders. Neuroses are the second most common group of psychiatric disturbances of childhood and symptoms include extreme anxiety related to over dependence, social isolation, sleep problems, unwarranted nausea, abdominal pain, diarrhea, or headaches. Some children show characteristics of irrational fears of particular objects or situations, while others become consumed with obsessions, thoughts, or ideas. One of the most serious neuroses is depression. The child is sad and depressed, crying, showing little or no interest in people or activities, having eating and sleeping problems, and sometimes talking about wanting to be dead. Teachers need to listen to what the child is saying and should take these verbal expressions very seriously.

Psychotic Disorders

An even more serious emotional disorder is psychosis which is characterized by a loss of contact with reality. Psychosis is rare in childhood but when it does occur, it is often difficult to diagnose. One fairly constant sign is the child's failure to make normal emotional contact with other people. The most common psychosis of childhood is schizophrenia which is a deliberate escape from reality and a withdrawal from relationships with others. When this syndrome occurs in childhood, the child will continue to have some contact with people, however; there is a curtain between them and the rest of the world. It is more common in boys than in girls. One of the major signs of this disorder is a habitually flat or habitually agitated facial expression. Children suffering from schizophrenia are occasionally mute, but at times they talk incessantly using bizarre words in ways that make no sense. Their incoherent speech often contributes to their frustration and compounds their fears and preoccupations and is the most significant sign of this very serious disturbance.

Early Infantile Autism

This disorder may occur as early as the fourth month of life. Suddenly the infant lies apathetic and oblivious in the crib. In other cases the baby seems perfectly normal throughout infancy and then the symptoms appear without warning at about eighteen months of age. Due to the nature of the symptoms, autistic children are often misdiagnosed as mentally retarded, deaf-mute, or organically brain-damaged. Autistic children are twice as likely to be boys as girls.

According to many psychologists who have been involved with treating autistic children, it seems that these children have built a wall between themselves and everyone else, including their families and even their parents. They do not make eye contact with others and do not even appear to hear the voices of those who speak to them. They cannot empathize with others and have no ability to appreciate humor.

Autistic children usually have language disturbances. One third of them never develops speech at all, but may grunt or whine. Others may repeat the same word or phrase over and over or parrot what someone else has said. They often lack even inner language as well and cannot play by themselves above a primitive, sensorimotor level.

Frequently autistic children will appear to fill the void left by the absence of interpersonal relationships in their lives with a preoccupation with things. They become compulsive about the arrangements of objects and often engage in simple, repetitive physical activities with objects for long periods of time. If these activities are interrupted, they may react with fear or rage. Others remain motionless for hours each day sometimes moving only their eyes or hands.

On intelligence tests, autistic children score from severely subnormal to high average. Some exhibit astonishing ability in isolated skill areas while functioning poorly in general. They may be able to memorize volumes of material, sing beautifully or perform complicated difficult mathematical problems.

The cause of early infantile autism is unknown. Years ago some psychiatrists speculated that these children did not develop normally due to a lack of parental warmth. This has been found to be unlikely since the incidence of autism in families is usually limited to one child. Other theories include metabolic or chromosomal defects as causes, but again, there is no proof.

The prognosis for autistic children is painfully discouraging. Only about five percent of autistic children become socially well-adjusted in adulthood. Another twenty percent make fair social adjustments. The remaining seventy-five percent are socially incapacitated and must be supervised for the duration of their lives. Treatment may include outpatient psychotherapy, drugs, or long-term treatment in a residential center, but neither the form of treatment nor even the lack of treatment seems to make a difference in the long run.

Skill 4.3   Recognizes intervention techniques that are appropriate for students whose overt behavior indicates severe emotional distress.

Many safe and helpful interventions are available to the classroom teacher when dealing with a student who is suffering serious emotional disturbances. First and foremost the teacher must maintain open communication with the parents and other professionals who are involved with the student whenever overt behavior characteristics are exhibited. Students with behavior disorders need constant behavior modification which may involve two way communication between the home and school on a daily basis.

The teacher must establish an environment that promotes appropriate behavior for all students as well as respect for one another. The students may need to be informed of any special needs that their classmates may have so that they can give due consideration. The teacher should also initiate a behavior modification program for any student that might show emotional or behavioral disorders. Such behavior modification plans can be effective means of preventing deviant behavior. If deviant behavior does occur, the teacher should have arranged for a safe and secure time-out place where the student can go for a respite and an opportunity to regain self-control.

Often when a behavior disorder is more severe, the student must be involved in a more concentrated program aimed at alleviating deviant behavior such as psychotherapy. In such instances, the school psychologist, guidance counselor, or behavior specialist is directly involved with the student and provides counseling and therapy on a regular basis. Frequently they are also involved with the student's family.

As a last resort, many families are turning to drug therapy. Once viewed as a radical step, administering drugs to children to balance their emotions or control their behavior has become a widely used form of therapy. Of course, only a medical doctor can prescribe such drugs. Great care must be exercised when giving pills to children in order to change their behavior, especially since so many medicines have undesirable side effects. It is important to know that these drugs relieve only the symptoms of behavior and do not get at the underlying causes. Parents need to be educated as to the side effects of these medications.

Skill 4.4   Knows and utilizes resources and procedures for referral of students.

One of the first things that a teacher learns is how to obtain resources and help for his/her students. All schools have guidelines for receiving this assistance especially since the implementation of the Americans with Disabilities Act. The first step in securing help is for the teacher to approach the school's administration or exceptional education department for direction in attaining special services or resources for qualifying students. Many schools have a committee designated for addressing these needs such as a Child Study Team or Core Team. These teams are made up of both regular and exceptional education teachers, school psychologists, guidance counselors, and administrators. The particular student's classroom teacher usually has to complete some initial paper work and will need to do some behavioral observations.

The teacher will take this information to the appropriate committee for discussion and consideration. The committee will recommend the next step to be taken. Often subsequent steps include a complete psychological evaluation along with certain physical examinations such as vision and hearing screening and a complete medical examination by a doctor.

The referral of students for this process is usually relatively simple for the classroom teacher and requires little more than some initial paper work and discussion. The services and resources that the student receives as a result of the process typically prove to be invaluable to the student with behavioral disorders.

At times, the teacher must go beyond the school system to meet the needs of some students. An awareness of special services and resources and how to obtain them is essential to all teachers and their students. When the school system is unable to address the needs of a student, the teacher often must take the initiative and contact agencies within the community. Frequently there is no special policy for finding resources. It is simply up to the individual teacher to be creative and resourceful and to find whatever help the student needs. Meeting the needs of all students is certainly a team effort which is most often spearheaded by the classroom teacher.

COMPETENCY 5.0   Recognizes signs of alcohol and drug abuse in students and demonstrates awareness of appropriate intervention and referral procedures.

It is first necessary to clarify abuse vs. dependency. Abuse is a lesser degree of involvement with substances, usually implying the person is not physically addicted. They may have just as many soft signs of involvement, but lack true addiction. Dependency indicates a true physical addiction, characterized by several hard signs, some of which are less likely to be seen in a school setting. The person may experience withdrawal symptoms when deprived of the substance. The person may experience blackouts. They may use more and more of the substance to get the same effect (tolerance). And they will exhibit irresponsible, illogical, and dangerous use of the substance. Soft signs, declines in functioning, are seen clearly in social, occupational, mental and emotional, and spiritual life. These last symptoms are most likely to be observed by an educator. Because determining addiction is not a concern for the educator, we will use the term abuse in this paper. The difference clinically may be academic for this age group, as addiction occurs at a high rate, and rapidly after first use in young people, sometimes after only a few tries. Legally, any use of an illicit substance for a minor, including alcohol, is automatically considered abuse.

Skill 5.1 Recognizes overt behaviors that may indicate a tendency toward the use of drugs and/or alcohol.

Discrimination is difficult here, due to the egregious behavioral problems encountered in the teenage world today that have nothing to do with substance abuse but mimic its traits. Predisposing behaviors indicating a tendency toward the use of drugs and/or alcohol usually are behaviors that suggest low self-esteem. Such might be academic failure, social maladaption, antisocial behavior, truancy, disrespect, chronic rule breaking, aggression and anger, and depression. The student tending toward the use of drugs and /or alcohol will exhibit losses in social and academic functional levels which were previously attained. He may begin to experiment with substances. The adage, "Pot makes a smart kid average and an average kid dumb," is right on the mark. There exist not a few families where pot smoking is a known habit of the parents. The children start their habit by stealing from the parents. Making it almost impossible to convince the child that drugs and alcohol are not good for them, parental use is hampering national efforts to clean up America.

Skill 5.2 Recognizes physical and behavioral characteristics of the youth who is abusing drugs and alcohol.

Typically, a student on drugs and/or alcohol will show:

muscle incoordination
wobbly, ataxic gait
reddened, puffy eyes (reddened
sclera)
averted gaze
dilated pupils
dry eyes
dry mouth (anticholinergia)
sneezing or sniffing excessively
and uncharacteristically
gazing off into space
nervousness
fine trembling
failure to respond to verbal
prompts
passive-aggressive behavior
sudden sickness in class
vomiting and chills
slurred speech
aggression
sleep
odd, sudden personality changes
withdrawal
an appearance of responding to internal stimuli
the smell of alcohol
or the smell of marijuana (pungent, sharp odor, similar to burning cane)
the appearance of powder around the nasal opening, on the clothes or hands

Skill 5.3 Uses immediate referrals when any student is suspected of using drugs and/or alcohol in order to protect other students and secure appropriate resistance for the offender.

There is a saying, "If you're going to be an alcoholic or drug addict in America, you will be." Cynical but true, this comment implies exposure to alcohol and drugs is 100%. We now have a wide-spread second generation of drug abusers in families. And alcohol is the oldest drug of abuse known to humankind, with many families affected for three and four or more known generations. It's hard to tell youth to eschew drugs when Mom and Dad, who grew up in the early illicit drug era, have a little toot or smoke and a few drinks on the weekends, or more often. Educators, therefore, are not only likely to, but often do face students who are high on something in school. Of course, they are not only a hazard to their own safety and those of others, but their ability to be productive learners is greatly diminished, if not non-existent. They show up instead of skip because it's not always easy or practical for them to spend the day away from home, but not in school. Unless they can stay inside they are at risk of being picked up for truancy. Some enjoy being high in school, having a sense of satisfaction getting over on the system. And for some, hardest to understand for some people, they just don't take drug use seriously enough to think usage at school might be inappropriate.

If it is questionable whether one should do the summoning, find out what the

protocol is on each step. Don't then notify the administration of the school center.

Seizures due to withdrawal are fatal 17% of the time. Overdoses due to mixed substances or overuse of a single substance are fatal, including overdoses with alcohol alone. Never under any circumstances attempt to treat, protect, tolerate, or negotiate with a student who is showing signs of a physical crisis. They are to be removed from the school center by EMS or police as soon as possible, and given constant one to one supervision away from the regular classroom before being taken to the hospital. A seriously impaired intoxicated student may leave school only if combative, uncontrollable and dangerous to approach. Police must be called nevertheless as this student is a danger to self or others in their condition.

Skill 5.4   Presents accurate information to students regarding tobacco, drug, and alcohol use.

Substance abuse of all kinds can be described by the following symptoms: Withdrawal syndrome, blackouts, and tolerance. These hard signs of addiction, or dependency, are those that affect physiology. 1) Withdrawal is seen when the substance(s) are removed and various symptoms indicating a metabolic craving are experienced: sweating, nausea, dizziness, elevated blood pressure, seizures, and rarely death. 2) When a substance dependent is seen ambulatory, but later doesn't remember anything of his actions, it's called a blackout. The anesthetized mind has eliminated conscious wakeful activity, functioning mainly on instinct. 3) Tolerance changes over the course of the disease, increasing in the early stages, and decreasing in the late chronic stage.

In the school setting, hard signs of dependency are to be considered very serious. Any student who exhibits hard signs associated with substance ingestion must be treated by medical staff at a medical facility immediately. Seizures due to withdrawal are fatal 17% of the time and overdoses due to mixed substances or overuse of a single substance are rapidly fatal, including overdoses with alcohol alone. Never under any circumstances attempt to treat, protect, tolerate, or negotiate with a student who is showing signs of a physical crisis. Always permit a seriously impaired intoxicated student to leave school when combative, uncontrollable and dangerous to approach. But police must be called as this student is a danger to self or others in their condition.

The abuser will show up more and more often unclean, unkempt, and disheveled. Actual style of clothes may change to more radical: nose rings, body piercing and tattoo work may follow. Outrageous appearance alone is not a symptom of substance abuse and is used by non-abusing youth, but there does seem to be a high correlation. The socially impaired substance abuser will frequently be late for school, for classes once in school, and other appointments. They seek less and less satisfaction from traditional social functions such as school athletics, rallies, plays, student government, and after school programs. Beware, some abusers use conformity in which to hide, and may be some of the most seriously impaired of all.

Another hard sign is: Irresponsible, Illogical, and Dangerous Use. The use of any substance by young people constitutes irresponsible, illogical and dangerous use, if for no other reason than substances of abuse, including alcohol, are all illegal. In the eyes of medical science and addictionology, there exists a zero level of tolerance because of the inherent physical risk ingesting street drugs, the possibility of brain damage, the loss of educational levels, and irreplaceably lost social development, diminishing a student's ability and chances in life. Psychologically, the use of drugs and alcohol prohibits the youth from struggling with non-chemical coping skills to solve problems. Typically, sophisticated anger modulation techniques usually learned in late adolescence are missed, leaving the person limited in handling that most important of emotions. Substance abuse is also dangerous, considering the terrible number of automobile crash deaths, teen pregnancies attained while intoxicated, overdose on contaminated substances, and the induction of mental disorders from exposure to harsh substances, such as activation of a latent schizophrenia by use of an hallucinogen.

There are three soft signs, less rapacious and life threatening, yet each a debilitating nightmare. They are the Three Psychosocial Declines. The young substance abuser will exhibit losses in functional levels socially and academically previously attained. The adage, "Pot makes a smart kid average and an average kid dumb," is right on the mark. There exist not a few families where pot smoking is a known habit of the parents. The children start their habit by stealing from the parents. Making it almost impossible to convince the child that drugs and alcohol are not good for them, parental use is hampering national efforts to clean up America.

Social Decline can be seen in the youth who is abusing drugs and alcohol. Typically he is one who, if known long enough by educators, will seem to be undergoing a personality change. Characteristically, social withdrawal is first noticed. The student fails to say hello, avoids being near teachers, seems evasive or sneaky, and associates with a lower status group than previously. Obviously, association with known substance abusers is almost always a warning sign. It is unacceptable when told they are just being friends with the known abuser, that they have other kinds of friends too. There is a sharp demarcation dividing both groups, and usually a young person doesn't straddle the line unless they intend to hop the fence once in a while ("If you hang around a barber shop, you're going to get a haircut"). The abuser will show up more and more often unclean, unkempt, disheveled. Actual style of clothes may change to more radical: nose rings, body piercing and tattoo work may follow. These alone are not symptoms of substance dependency, and are used by non-abusing youth, but they are almost always found in a company of substance abusers. The socially impaired substance abuser will frequently be late for school, for classes once in school, and other appointments. They seek less and less satisfaction from traditional social functions such as school athletics, rallies, plays, student government, and after school programs. Beware, some abusers use conformity in which to hide, and may be some of the most seriously impaired of all.

Mental and Emotional Impairment manifests as the disease deepens its grip. Declining academic scores and standardized test scores; loss of interest in school, failure to respond quickly to prompts, sharp noises, or sudden actions, emotional flattening or liability, personality changes, vacant personality, hyperactivity, depression, suicide talk and attempts, psychosis, and a motivation characterize mental and emotional impairments due to substance abuse. And then there are those students, already having emotional problems (about 3-6% of any given population of youth), who are more vulnerable to using drugs and alcohol than well adjusted ones. Caution is recommended when questioning teenagers who might have another psychiatric illness that you aren't aware of. They may present looking like they are high. But they may be reacting to medications. Or their odd behavior may be due to the psychiatric illness itself, not substance abuse. Knowing a student's history, if available, helps.

Finally comes Spiritual Decline, an even less obvious manifestation than the previously mentioned signs. By spiritual, the broadest usage is the youth's existential relationship to the greater world around him. Attitudes of respect, humility, wonder and affection indicate a person who has a sense of relationship to something greater at large. Attitudes of contempt, pride, ignorance, and arrogance indicate one who lacks an awareness of the enormity of existence. More specifically, a previously religious or reverent student may suddenly become blatantly disrespectful of organized religion. The inappropriate use of the cross or other religious symbol frequently indicates spiritual decline. The person experiencing this decline is lost to his own devices. He hasn't a foundation of faith in anything other than himself getting high to make it through when times are rough. Perhaps it is the presence or absence of faith that best defines this area of loss.

Students are using drugs and alcohol at surprisingly young ages today. Cases exist of ten year old alcoholics. Young people start using drugs and alcohol for one of four reasons:

1) out of curiosity, 2) to party, 3) from peer pressure, 4) to avoid dealing with problems. Intervention is failing today in the last item. Almost every student understands the dangers of drug and alcohol usage. But there are those hard core users who can't

resist involvement because their emotional pain is so high. The causes are many in today's complex world, not the least of which is family and community breakdown. The family is typically 50% a blended family today, with a similar national divorce rate. Children are transported from parent to parent, often against their own wishes. Ex-spouses are not always successful at avoiding retaliating against each other through children. Children from these families feel guilt, anger, and shame, usually unresolved. Once considered relatively harmless to children, divorce is now being re-evaluated as probably the most serious harm of all to children. These children, 50% of our school population, are more prone to substance abuse than others. Other problems that cause students to have emotional pain include social awkwardness, depression, incipient major mental illnesses, personality disorders, learning disabilities, ADHD, conduct disorder, and substance abuse and dependency in family members. The most common emotional problem found in student populations is parent-child problem, descriptively naming a deficit in communication, authority, and respect between parent and child. A close second is conduct disorder, a behavior set characterized by aggression, exploitation, violence, disregard for the rights of others, animal cruelty, fire setting, enuresis, defiance, running away, truancy, juvenile arrest record, and associated ADHD, substance abuse, and parent-child problem.

A national appetite for drugs and alcohol, the dismal performance of drug interdiction policies and campaigns, and a lack of social services, including those which might be provided in school centers, perpetuates substance abuse in these young people, dooming many of them to tragic lives of loss, incompetence, underclass status, and often death.

If the reader has become saddened or upset by what they've read so far, the following will do nothing to appease. In youth, there exists two beliefs, almost universally held, functional and adaptive in many settings, but devastating to the young person about to get involved in substance abuse. They have been called the Twin Dragons of Substance Abuse and Dependency. One dragon, standing guard on the right, tells the student, "YOU HAVE NOTHING TO LOSE!" supported by an awareness of having few possessions, no career, no wife and kids, little to live for, nothing to die for. This risk-taking belief is adaptive and functional for the young person who wants to take off for a solo sail around the world, or design the newest and best computer program ever, or travel to meet the Dalai Lama. For the substance abuse adventurer, it's deadly. The other dragon, guarding the left flank, whispers hotly into the students head, "NOTHING CAN HURT YOU!"

Invulnerability is highly adaptive, considering a historic period when people needed fearlessness at a young age. To die for God and King was once a pretty noble idea. The young knight, not much older than our high school student, set forth with the brash pride and bravado that only Cause can give. Against the insidiousness of crack rock, the bold attitudes crumble to ash.

These twin delusions have to be smashed before the young person can ever see the truth. They must learn dependency on people when the drug demands allegiance.

Substance abuse and dependency in young people are treatable illnesses, but must be recognized as such and taken seriously. Even abuse must be forbidden, and dependency aggressively treated. The worst nightmare our nation would ever have to face is if these were ever considered normative.

COMPETENCY 6.0 **Recognizes the overt physical and behavioral indicators of child abuse and neglect, knows the rights and responsibilities regarding reporting and how to interact appropriately with a child after a report has been made.**

Skill 6.1 Recognizes physical, mental, emotional and social behavioral indicators of child abuse and neglect.

Child abuse may perpetuate itself in a phenomenon known as chronic shock. The system becomes geared up to handle the extra flow of hormones and electrical impulses accompanying the "fight or flight" syndrome each time the abuse happens, creating a permanent shift in the biology of the brain and allied systems. Essentially, the victim becomes allergic (hypersensitized) to stress of the kind which prevailed during the period of abuse. Recent research indicates such a shift is reflected in brain chemistry and structural changes and lasts a lifetime.

The abused child differs from the neglected one. While the neglected child suffers from understimulation, the abused one suffers from over-stimulation. The neglected child will be withdrawn, quiet, unanticipating, sedate almost, while the abused child may be angry, energetic, rebellious, aggressive, and hard to control. In each case, the environment of abuse or neglect shapes the behavior of the child away from home. Often, out of reflex, the child will flinch when seeming to anticipate a blow, or be unable to accept or understand healthy attention directed to him. The teacher merely needs to watch the child's reaction to a sudden loud noise, another child's aggression, or the response when offered some companionship by another child, or test their own feelings to sense what the child's feelings and experiences may be.

The affective range of the abused and/or neglected child varies from very limited and expressionless to angry, to a distracted effect that is characterized by inattentiveness and poor concentration. Some are tearful, some angry and hitting, and some are just sedentary. In most cases, the effect displayed will not be appropriate to the situation at hand. They have just too much to think about in their mind, their sense of powerlessness is too strong, and unable to tell the terrible tale, they may block it out or become obsessed by it.

The obvious thing the teacher sees are marks from the hand, fist, belt, coat hangers, kitchen utensils, extension cord, and any other imaginable implement for striking and inflicting pain on a child. Now, the suspicion has to be backed up with hard evidence. Unusual marks in geometric shapes may indicate the presence of an implement for spanking such as a spoon, home-made paddle, extension cord, or coat hanger. Marks on the arms and legs may indicate being whipped there. Always be suspicious about bruising. Bruises on the neck and face are usually not the result of a trip and fall, but have a lot to do with intentional hitting, and even choking. Noting the size and shapes of bruises and using some simple imagination may reveal the source of the injury. Notice whether the bruise has reddened areas, indicating ruptured capillaries, or is uniformly colored but shaded toward the perimeter. The rupture of capillaries indicates a strong hit while the shaded bruise indicates a softer compression. The job of the educator who discovers this is just to have a reasonable suspicion that abuse is going on, but it helps to have some specific indicators and firm evidence, not only for the sake of the child, but in the rare event that your report is questioned.

The neglected child may appear malnourished, may gorge at lunch, yet still be thin and underweight. Quiet and shy, he's typically shabby looking, and doesn't seem to care about his appearance. Poor nutrition at home may result in him having more than his share of colds and it is of utmost importance to guarantee that his immunizations are current, as they probably have been overlooked. He is not usually a very social child, may isolate, and not respond to invitations to join in. Many children display this trait, but a persistence in social anxiety with a sad effect will indicate that something is happening at home to be concerned about.

In cases of sexual abuse the most blatant warning sign is the sexualization of the child. They become interested in matters of sexuality way before their development stage would predict. They are sexual. They may be seen to quietly masturbate in school at prepubertal ages, and may even act out sexually with other children of their own age. The child who suddenly begins to engage in promiscuous sexual behavior is likely to have been molested. Sexual abuse of children is widespread and takes many forms. Kissing episodes by a parent, when out of normal context, are just as damaging as more overt forms of contact, as is the sexualized leer or stare by a perverted parent or elder. Because of the complexity of dealing with sexual abuse, situations must be dealt with extremely carefully. Never attempt an exhaustive interview of a student who admits to being sexually abused, or abused in any way, but wait for the trained professional who knows the methodology to help out. The outcome of an interview can make or break a prosecution.

Skill 6.2 Knows the rights and responsibilities of all parties involved and the procedure for reporting abuse/neglect incidents.

The child who is undergoing the abuse is the one whose needs must be served first. A suspected case gone unreported may destroy a child's life, and their subsequent life as a functional adult. It is the duty of any citizen who suspects abuse and neglect to make a report, and it is especially important and required for State licensed and certified persons to make a report. All reports can be kept confidential if required, but it is best to disclose your identity in case more information is required of you. This is a personal matter which has no impact on qualifications for licenser or certification. Failure to make a report when abuse or neglect is suspected is punishable by revocation of certification and license, a fine, and criminal charges.

It is the right of any accused individual to have counsel and make a defense, as in any matter of law. The procedure for reporting makes clear the rights of the accused, who stands before the court innocent until proven guilty, with the right to representation, redress and appeal, as in all matters of United States law. The State is cautious about receiving spurious reports, but investigates any that seem real enough. Some breaches of standards of decency are not reportable offenses, such as possession of pornography which is not hidden from children. But go ahead and make the report and let the counselor make the decision. Your conscience is clear, and you have followed all procedures which keep you from liability. Your obligation to report is immediate when you suspect abuse.

There is no time given as an acceptable or safe period of time to wait before reporting, so hesitation to report may be a cause for action against you. Do not wait once your suspicion is firm. All you need to have is a reasonable suspicion, not actual proof, which is the job for the investigators. The State of Florida Department of Health and Rehabilitative Services maintains the abuse hotelmen, 1-800-962-2873, for 24 hours a day reporting. The counselor answering the call will determine if your case needs immediate attention or attention within the next 24 hours. If immediate response is required a team is sent on the spot. Otherwise, they will put the case on a visit basis within 24 hours.

Skill 6.3 Knows how to interact appropriately based on the child's needs after a child abuse/neglect report has been made.

Interaction after the report has been made is always optional on the part of the teacher. The student will need to feel supported and not betrayed, so if their confidence was damaged to make the report, it should be explained that it was necessary for their protection, and that it is regretted if they are further hurt due to it, but something had to be done. The apology is not meant for the act of reporting, but for any complications the child feels due it. It may make the child more comfortable about fearing retaliation if he knows that the adult who made the report is aware that it might happen. The child needs to believe that the adults in his world are trustworthy, even though some have let him down. And he needs to have an avenue of recourse if the abuse continues or if he is acted on for reporting.

Interaction with State agencies is always mandatory subsequent to a report. For simple data gathering, the process should be uncomplicated. If a case goes legal, then the teacher may wish to be protected by counsel. The rights of one who reports in good faith are protected, but with unanticipated twists and turns in law the concept of self protection is advised. The teacher is never advised to speak to the alleged perpetrators. The act of reporting needs no defense if there is no offense against the child. Anyone who is not guilty can withstand an investigation. Safeguards are built into the system to prevent its abuse. But avoiding the alleged perpetrator is strongly recommended, and if a situation of harassment or persecution arises, it must be dealt with immediately through the local police.

Last, in cases of child sexual abuse, the boundaries and limits which normally protect a child from having to deal with complicated adult sexuality have been violated. It is always recommended to not touch the child in any but the most cautious and sensitive manner, aware of the sense of violation they may feel. In many cases it is all right to ask the child if you may touch or hold hands. Don't force the issue. Simply respect their wishes if they decline, knowing that it has to do with the perpetrator, not you, and that someday they may say yes. Keep trying to draw this child out, as isolation and withdrawal are common sequel. If you are interviewing the child for the first preliminary date, keep your inquiry short, respecting any privacy or secrecy they may present with. Eventually, with the trained experts, they will be able to break silence. Your work prior to the actual investigations is crucial to a satisfactory outcome.

COMPETENCY 7.0 Formulate a standard for student behavior in the classroom.

Skill 7.1   Identifies approved safety procedures, student characteristics socially accepted norms (such as mutual respect, consideration of others, courtesy) and incorporates them into a standard for student behavior in the classroom.

Establish a plan for social skills development.

Teaching social skills can be rather difficult because social competence requires a repertoire of skills in a number of areas. The socially competent person must be able to get along with family and friends, function in a work environment, take care of personal needs, solve problems in daily living, and identify sources of help. A class of emotionally handicapped students may present several deficits in a few areas or a few deficits in many areas. Therefore, the teacher must begin with an assessment of the skill deficits and prioritize the ones to teach first.

Social skills instruction can include teaching for conversation skills, assertiveness, play and peer interaction, problem solving and coping skills, self-help, task-related behaviors, self-concept related skills (i.e., expressing feelings, accepting consequences), and job related skills.

Type of Assessment   Description
Direct Observation Observe student in various settings with a checklist
Role Play   Teacher observes students in structured scenarios
Teacher Ratings   Teacher rates student with a checklist or formal assessment instrument
Sociometric Measures:
Peer Nomination

Peer Rating

Paired-Comparison Student names specific classmates who meet a stated criterion (i.e., playmate). Score is the number of times a child is nominated.

Students rank all their classmates on a Likert-type scale (e.g., 1-3 or 1-5 scale) on stated criterion. Individual score is the average of the total ratings of their classmates.

Student is presented with paired classmate combinations and asked to choose who is most or least liked in the pair. Context Observation Student is observed to determine if the skill deficit is present one setting, but not others. Comparison with other student's social skill behavior is compared to two other students in the same situation to determine if there is a deficit, or if the behavior is not really a problem.

Skill 7.2 States expectations about student conduct, giving rules or developing them with student's, and illustrating rules for clarification.

About 4 to 6 classroom rules should be posted where students can easily see and read them. These rules should be stated positively, and describe specific behaviors so that they are easy to understand. Certain rules may also be tailored to meet target goals and IEP requirements of individual students. (For example, a new student who has had problems with leaving the classroom may need an individual behavior contract to assist him or her with adjusting to the class rule about remaining in the assigned area.)

Rules should be established right away when a teacher receives a new group of students. Students should be involved as much as possible in the formulation of the rules and discuss why the rules are necessary. When students get involved in helping establish the rules, they will be more likely to assume responsibility for following them. Once the rules are established, enforcement and reinforcement for following the rules should begin right away.

The teacher should clarify and model the expected behavior for the students. In addition to the classroom management plan, a management plan should be developed for special situations, (i.e., fire drills) and transitions (i.e. going to and from the cafeteria). Periodic review of the rules, as well as modeling and practice, may be conducted as needed, such as after an extended school holiday.

Consequences should be introduced when the rules are introduced, clearly stated, and understood by all of the students. The severity of the consequence should match the severity of the offense and must be enforceable. The teacher must apply the consequence consistently and fairly; so that the students will know what to expect when they choose to break a rule.

Like consequences, students should understand what rewards to expect for following the rules. The teacher should never promise a reward which cannot be delivered, and follow through with the reward as soon as possible. Consistency and fairness is also necessary for rewards to be effective. Students will become frustrated and give up if they see that rewards and consequences are not delivered timely and fairly.

Develop success-oriented activities.

Success-oriented activities are tasks that are selected to meet the individual needs of the student. During the time a student is learning a new skill, tasks should be selected so that the student will be able to earn a high percentage of correct answers during the teacher questioning and seatwork portions of the lesson. Later, the teacher should also include work that challenges students to apply what they have learned and stimulate their thinking.

Skill knowledge, strategy use, motivation, and personal interests are all factors that influence individual student success. The student who can't be bothered with reading the classroom textbook may be highly motivated to read the driver's handbook for his or her license, or the rule book for the latest video game. Students who did not master their multiplication tables will likely have problems working with fractions.

In the success-oriented classroom, mistakes are viewed as a natural part of the learning process. The teacher can demonstrate the learning power of mistakes by purposely including mistakes in the lesson and modeling the thinking process of correcting the error. The teacher can also show that adults make mistakes by correcting errors without getting unduly upset. The students feel safe to try new things because they know that they have a supportive environment and can correct their mistakes.

Activities that promote student success:
♦ Are based on useful, relevant content that is clearly specified, and organized for easy learning.

♦ Allow sufficient time to learn the skill and is selected for high rate of success.

♦ Allows students the opportunity to work independently, self-monitor, and set goals.

♦ Provide for frequent monitoring and corrective feedback.

♦ Include collaboration in group activities or peer teaching.

Students with learning problems often attribute their successes to luck or ease of the task. Their failures are often blamed on their supposed lack of ability, difficulty of the task, or the fault of someone else. Successful activities, attribution retraining, and learning strategies can help these students to discover that they can become independent learners. When the teacher communicates the expectation that the students can be successful learners and chooses activities that will help them be successful, achievement is increased.

Develop a plan for progression from directed to self-directed activity.

Learning progresses in stages from initial acquisition, when the student needs a lot of teacher guidance and instruction to adaptation, when the student can apply what he or she has learned to new situations outside the classroom. As students progress through the stages of learning, the teacher gradually decreases the amount of direct instruction and guidances and encourages the student to function independently. The ultimate goal of the learning process is to teach students how to be independent and apply their knowledge. A summary of these states and their features appears here:

State Teacher Activity   Emphasis
Initial Acquisition   Provide rationale Guidance, Demonstration
Modeling
Shaping
Cueing   Errorless learning
Backward Chaining (working from the final product backward through the steps)
Forward Chaining (proceeding through the steps to a final product)
Advanced Acquisition   Feedback
Error correction
Specific directions
        Criterion evaluation
Reinforcement and reward for accuracy
Proficiency   Positive reinforcement
Progress monitoring
Teach self-management
Increased teacher expectations   Increase speed or performance to the automatic level with accuracy
Set goals
Self-management
Maintenance Withdraw direct reinforcement
Retention and memory
Overlearning
Intermittent schedule of reinforcement   Maintain high level of performance
Mnemonic techniques
Social and intrinsic reinforcement
Generalization   Corrective feedbackPerform skill in different times and places
Adaptation   Stress independent problem-solving   Independent problem-solving methods
No direct guidance or direct instruction

Adapt for transitions.

Transitions refers to changes in class activities which involve movement. Examples are (a) breaking up from large group instruction into small groups for learning centers and small-group instructions, (b) classroom to lunch, to the playground, or to elective classes, (c) finishing reading at the end of one period and getting ready for math the next period and (d) emergency situations such as fire drills. Successful transitions are achieved by using proactive strategies. Early in the year, the teacher pinpoints the transition periods in the day and anticipates possible behavior problems, such as students habitually returning late from lunch. After identifying possible problems with the environment or the schedule, the teacher plans proactive strategies to minimize or eliminate those problems. Proactive planning also gives the teacher the advantage of being prepared, addressing behaviors before they become problems, and incorporating strategies into the classroom management plan right away.

Transition plans can be developed for each type of transition and the expected behaviors for each situation taught directly to the students.

A. **Identify the specific behaviors are needed for the type of transition**. For example, during a fire drill, students must quickly leave the classroom, walk quietly as a group to the designated exit, proceed to the assigned waiting area, stay with the group, wait for the teacher to receive the all=clear signal, walk quickly and quietly back to the classroom with the group, and re-enter the classroom and return to the seat. Transition to the cafeteria is similar in the walking procedure, but is different in that cafeteria behavior involves waiting in line for food without cutting, pushing, or bothering others in line, leaving the table area clean and neat, putting trays in the designated area, and perhaps sitting at an assigned table. For each situation, the teacher needs to decide what the student will be expected to do, as well as what possible problems to expect.

B. **Develop a set of expectations and teach them to the students**. The expected behaviors should be written in a positive, specific language. Establish a rationale for the rules and provide an explanation of the rules. Provide corrective feedback and reinforcement to the students who demonstrate knowledge of the rules.

C. **Model the appropriate behavior.** Guide the students through the procedures and give reinforcement to those who correctly model the behavior.

D. **Have the students practice the behaviors independently** and continue corrective feedback and reinforcement. Certain situations, like the fire drill, will not be practiced on a daily basis, but students will have daily opportunities to demonstrate appropriate transition behavior in and out of class.

Skill 7.3   Identifies and incorporates local and state policies into a standard for student behavior in the classroom.

Develop a behavior management plan.

Guided by local and state policies for behavior management plans the teacher may be write plans for a group or an individual. Behavior management techniques should focus on positive procedures that can be used at home as well at school. When an intervention is needed, the least restrictive method should be used first, except in severe situations (i.e., fighting, dangerous behaviors). For example, a child who begins talking instead of working in class would not be immediately placed into time out, because the teacher can use less intrusive techniques to prompt the child to return to task. The teacher could use a signal or verbal prompt to gain the child's attention, then praise him when he is back on task, for example.

The School Board of Palm Beach County, for example, has developed a policy for the use of behavior management procedures with ESE students in order to develop consistency in the types of procedures used, methods of applying those procedures, training staff, and compliance with IEP guidelines.

Valid Interventions
(Positive in Nature)
Do not require parent notification when used   Category I Examples
(Mildly Restrictive)
Require parent notification when used   Category II Examples
(Restrictive)
Require parent notification when used
Use of 3 interventions required before using a higher-level and must include these components: Response Cost—loss of privilege or reward   Spaced Eating Program—used with treatment for eating disorders such as rumination/regurgitation
1. A differential reinforcement procedure:
(a) Differential Reinforcement for Other Behaviors (DRO)
(b) Differential Reinforcement for Incompatible Behaviors (DRI)
(c) Differential Reinforcement for Alternative Behaviors (DRA)   Contingent observation—student watches others get rewards for appropriate behavior Inhibiting devices—used to reduce serious self-injurious behaviors (SIBS)
2. Schedules of Reinforcement   Exclusion Time-out at seat with no social or tangible reward for misbehavior

Mechanical Restraints--may be used for SIBS or as a protective device for support with a physically impaired student

3. Attempt to determine the functional analysis of the behavior. (What possible factors in the child's environment may be causing or reinforcing the behavior?)   Overcorrection--student fixes the results of his misbehavior and improves the environment   All of the above require the recommendation and/or approval of a physician

4. Intervention should be predominantly positive.   Contingent Negative Substances-- used to reduce SIBS, biting, or pica when safety of child or others is at risk. Examples: water mist, lemon juice therapy, oral hygiene overcorrection

Procedures that use social humiliation, withholding of basic needs, pain, or extreme discomfort should never be used in a behavior management plan. Emergency intervention procedures used when the student is a danger to himself or others are not considered behavior management procedures. Throughout the year, the teacher should periodically review the types of interventions being used, assess the effectiveness of the interventions used in the management plan, and make revisions as needed for the best interests of the child.

Classroom management plans should be in place when the school year begins. Developing a management plan takes a proactive approach--that is, decide what behaviors will be expected of the class as a whole, anticipate possible problems, and teach the behaviors early in the school year. Involving the students in the development of the classroom rules lets the students know the rationale for the rules, allows them to assume responsibility in the rules because they had a part in developing them.

Just as with the transition plan, the classroom behavior management plan should be taught with the teacher establishing the rationale and explaining the rules, demonstrating examples and non-examples of the expected behaviors, and guiding the students through practice of the behaviors. As the students demonstrate the behaviors, the teacher should provide reinforcement and corrective feedback. Periodic "refresher" practice can be done as needed, for example, after a long holiday or if students begin to "slack off". A copy of the classroom plan should be readily available for substitute use, and the classroom aide should also be familiar with the plan and procedures.

The development of a class or individual behavior management plan proceeds through several phases :

1. Selecting and defining the target behavior. The target behavior may be one that the teacher would like to decrease (e.g., call-outs, out-of-seat, late to class), increase (answering questions in class, completing homework assignments), or develop (volunteering answers in class, raising hand to speak, neat table manners at lunch).

Target behaviors may be for academic or social skills.

Often there are several behaviors that could be target behaviors. When that is the case, consider the behaviors in terms of their frequency, rate, duration, intensity, and type. Another consideration is the degree of unacceptability of the behavior. For example, gum chewing, tardiness, and cursing in class are all unacceptable school behaviors. Gum chewing would have the lowest priority as a target behavior because it creates the least social and academic problem for the student. In the case of the student's cursing or being late to class, the teacher would need to decide which at the moment is more of a problem. If the student frequently curses and disrupts the class, then the cursing would take priority. If the student occasionally curses, but is chronically late to class because he has been wandering around socializing, then the tardy behavior would take priority.

Selecting target behaviors may also be a function of what others perceive as unacceptable or their degree of tolerance for the behavior. What one teacher finds greatly unacceptable may not be so terrible to another. Behaviors that occur infrequently or do not usually interfere with class may be addressed by the classroom management plan and not need an individual plan. However, behaviors that interfere with the child's functioning or threaten the safety of the student and others obviously need modification. *A key point is to consider is how the behavior affects the functioning of the individual as well as the classroom setting.* In some cases, the behavior may be well within normal child behavior for a certain age or developmental phase.

2. Collecting baseline information. Generally data collection is done for a 3 to 5 day period, but may be extended if necessary. The target behavior must be observable, measurable, and specifically defined in behavioral terms so that the behavior is accurately recorded. Depending on the behavior, the teacher may simply tally the *frequency* of the behavior (i.e., number of times late to class in a week's time, times out of seat during a class period). *Duration recording* may be used for measuring the time a behavior lasts (i.e., temper tantrum, time spent out of seat). *Latency recording* is used to measure the time between a stimulus and a behavior (i.e., a question and an answer). If the teacher is observing several students, then *interval recording* may be the method of choice. The results should be charted or graphed for ease in analysis. By charting the course of a behavior, the teacher can analyze how often a behavior occurs, if there are patterns to the behavior (i.e., certain times of the day, or getting "sick" on the days the class has P.E., but not on the days the art teacher has class). Other ways of collecting information include reviews of cumulative or anecdotal records, interviews with the child or an adult, or analyzing another person's data.

3. Choosing suitable reinforcers. A key point here is that *what the teacher, classmate, or parent considers desirable is not necessarily the child's idea of a suitable reinforcer.*

The teacher can find out what the child likes or dislikes by using a commercially prepared Likert-type scale or a teacher-prepared interview. Often direct observation will show what the child chooses for a reinforcer. The reinforcers may be presented at school or in conjunction with a plan between the parent, student, and teacher. Other considerations for choice of reinforcers may be the ability to deliver the reinforcer at school, suitability of the reinforcer, or school policy (for example, a teacher would not want to reward a student with gum if gum is not allowed at school).

4. Transition from tangible to intrinsic reinforcers. A variety of reinforcers should be available to maintain student interest prevent boredom. This "menu" can also include potential reinforcers. Tangible reinforcers, especially food, should be gradually mixed with social and intangible reinforcers, with the eventual goal to fade out tangible to social reinforcers. This is accomplished by presenting both types initially on a fixed schedule, then maintaining the social reinforcers on a fixed schedule and making the tangibles on a variable schedule, and finally presenting the social reinforcers on a variable schedule.

Categories and General Examples of Reinforcers

Type Examples
Tangible, Consumable Food   Fruit, raisins, candies, juice, soda, popcorn, chips (Check for allergies or food reactions first.)
Tangible Non-Food Pens, Pencils, "school store", movie passes
Tokens   Stars, stickers, award certificates
Games   Board games, blocks, puzzles, dolls
Activity   Movies, free time, field trips, listen to music
Social (Intrinsic)   Praise, hugs, being in charge of an activity, visiting with a friend
Jobs Cafeteria helper, office aide, errands for teachers, classroom chores

5. Selecting and implementing the intervention. Choice of intervention depends on whether the target behavior is selected for increase, decrease, development, or maintenance. The length of time the intervention is applied will vary, depending on the effectiveness of the intervention. The intervention should be applied for a sufficient number of days before deciding to stop or try something else. This is because some negative behaviors (i.e., hitting, crying to get one's way) may initially increase as the child sees that the results are not what he or she is used to getting through the behavior.

Skill 7.4 Implements rules and maintains a standard of conduct.

Behavior Management Plan Strategies for Increasing Desired Behaviors

1. *Prompt--A visual or verbal cue that assists the child through the behavior shaping process.* In some cases, the teacher may use a physical prompt such as guiding a child's hand. Visual cues include signs or other visual aids. Verbal cues include talking a child through the steps of a task. *The gradual removal of the prompt as the child masters the target behavior is called fading.*

2. Modeling--In order for modeling to be effective, the child must first be at a cognitive and developmental level to imitate the model.. Teachers are behavior models in the classroom, but peers are powerful models as well, especially in adolescence. A child who does not perceive a model as acceptable will not likely copy the model's behavior. This is why teachers should be careful to reinforce appropriate behavior and not fall into the trap of attending to inappropriate behaviors. Children who see that the students who misbehave get the teacher's constant attention will most likely begin to model those students' behaviors.

3. Contingency Contracting. *(Also known as the Premack Principle or "Grandma's Law").* This technique is based on the concept that a preferred behavior that frequently occurs can be used to increase a less preferred behavior with a low rate of occurrence. In short, performance of X results in the opportunity to do Y, such as getting 10 minutes of free time for completing the math assignment with 85% accuracy,

Contingency contracts are a process that continues after formal schooling and into the world of work and adult living. Contracts can be individualized, developed with input of the child, and accent positive behaviors. Contingencies can also be simple verbal contracts, such as the teacher telling a child that he or she may earn a treat or special activity for completion of a specific academic activity. Contingency contracts can be simple daily contracts or more formal, written contracts.

Written contracts last for longer periods of time, and must be clear, specific, and fair. Payoffs should be deliverable immediately after the student completes the terms of the contract. An advantage of a written contract is that the child can see and re-affirm the terms of the contract. By being actively involved in the development of the contract with the teacher and/or parent, the child assumes responsibility for fulfilling his share of the deal. Contracts can be renewed and renegotiated as the student progresses toward the target behavior goal.

4. Token Economy. A token economy mirrors our money system in that the students earn tokens ("money") which are of little value in themselves, but can be traded for tangible or activity rewards, just as currency can be spent for merchandise. Using stamps, stickers,

stars, or point cards instead of items like poker chips decrease the likelihood of theft, loss, and noise in the classroom.

Tips for a token economy:

♦ Keep the system simple to understand and administer
♦ Develop a reward "menu" which is deliverable and varied
♦ Decide on the target behaviors
♦ Explain the system completely and in positive terms before beginning the economy
♦ Periodically review the rules
♦ Price the rewards and costs fairly, and post the menu where it will be easily read.
♦ Gradually fade to a variable schedule of reinforcement

Skill 7.5 Monitors compliance and non-compliance with classroom rules and provides consequences to increase appropriate and decrease inappropriate behaviors

Behavior Management Plan Strategies for Decreasing Undesirable Behaviors

1. *Extinction*--Reinforcement is withheld for an unacceptable behavior. A common example is ignoring the student who calls out without raising his hand and recognizing the student who is raising his hand to speak. This would not be a suitable strategy for serious misbehaviors where others are in danger of being hurt.

2. *Differential Reinforcement of Incompatible Behaviors (DRI)*.--In this method, the teacher reinforces an acceptable behavior that is not compatible with the target behavior. A child cannot be out of her seat and in her seat at the same time, so the teacher would reinforce the time when the child is in her seat.

3. *Differential Reinforcement of Alternative Behaviors (DRA)*.--Student is reinforced for producing a behavior which is an alternative to the undesired target behavior, such as talking with a classmate instead of arguing.

4. *Differential Reinforcement of Other Behaviors (DRO)*.--Reinforcement is provided for producing any appropriate behaviors except for the target behavior during a specified time interval. This technique works well with stereotypic, disruptive, or self-injurious behaviors.

5. *Satiation or Negative Practice.*--This technique involves reinforcing the inappropriate behavior on a fixed reinforcement schedule until the student discontinues the behavior. The reinforcement must be consistently applied until the student does not want to do it. Behaviors suitable for satiation would be chronic "borrowing" of school supplies, getting up to go to the wastebasket or pencil sharpener, or asking for the time. An example would be giving a student a pencil to sharpen at frequent intervals throughout the day so that the act of getting up to sharpen a pencil no longer has any appeal.

6. *Verbal Reprimands.* Reprimands are best delivered privately, especially for secondary students, who may be provoked into more misbehavior if they are embarrassed in front of their peers. Verbal reprimands also may be a source of attention and reinforcement with some students.

Punishment as a " Deterrent" to Misbehavior

Punishment should **not** be the first strategy in behavior management plans because it tends to suppress behavior, not eliminate it. Punishment focuses on the negative rather than positive behaviors. There is also the chance that the child will comply out of fear, stress, or tension rather than a genuine behavior change. Furthermore, there is the chance that punishment may be misused to the point where it is no longer effective. Forms or punishment include:

1. *Adding an aversive event* (i.e., detention, lunchroom cleanup, extra assignments, spanking)

2. *Subtracting something that the child likes* (Television privileges, recess, dessert).

3. *Response Cost.* In token economies response cost results in loss of points or token.. Response-cost or loss of privileges is preferred to adding aversives, but for long-term changes in behavior, punishment is less effective than other forms of decreasing misbehavior, such as extinction and ignoring.

4. *Time-Out*—Time-out means removing a child from the reinforcing situation to a setting which is not reinforcing. Time out may be **observational** (i.e., sitting at the end of the basketball court for 5 minutes or putting one's head down at the desk). The point is to have the child observe the others engaging in the appropriate behavior. **Exclusion time-out** involves placing a visual barrier between the student and the rest of the class. This could be a divider between the desks and the time-out area, or removing the child to another room. **Seclusion time-out** necessitates a special time-out room which adheres to mandated standards, as well as a log of the children who are taken to time out, the reasons, and the time spent there.

In order to be effective, time-out must be consistently applied, and the child must know why he is being sent to the time out area and for how long. The teacher briefly explain the reason for time-out, direct the child to the area, and refrain from long explanations, arguments, or debates. The time-out area should be as neutral as possible, away from busy areas, and easily observed by the monitor, but not from the rest of the class. The duration of time-out should vary with the age of the child, and timed so the child knows when the end of time-out has arrived.

Time-out as part of a behavior management plan needs to be periodically evaluated for its effectiveness. By analyzing records of time-out (as required and directed by the school district), the teacher can see if the technique is working. If a student regularly goes to time-out at a certain time, the student may be avoiding a frustrating situation or a difficult academic subject. Seclusion time out may be effective for children who tend to be group-oriented, acting-out, or aggressive. Isolation from the group is not rewarding for them. Shy, solitary, or withdrawn children may actually prefer to be in time-out and increase the target behavior in order to go to time-out.

6. *Overcorrection:* Overcorrection is more effective with severe and profoundly handicapped students. The student is required to repeat an appropriate behavior for a specified number of times when the inappropriate behavior is exhibited.

7. *Suspension* is the punishment of last resort. In addition to restrictions on suspension for students with disabilities, suspension translates into a "vacation" from school for many students with behavioral problems. Furthermore, suspension does not relieve the teacher from the responsibility of exploring alternatives which may be effective with the child. An alternative to out-of-school suspension is in-school suspension, where the student is placed in a special area to do his or her classwork for a specified time and with minimal privileges. Extended suspensions, i.e., for drugs, weapons, or assault) or offenses punishable by expulsion result in a change of placement, which calls for special meetings to discuss alternative placement and/or services

Group-Oriented Contingencies in Behavior Management

This strategy uses the power of the peer group to reinforce appropriate behavior. In one variation, *dependent group-oriented contingencies*, the rewards of consequences for the entire group depend upon the performance of a few members. Example: Susan's class receives a candy reward if she does not have a crying outburst for two days. *Interdependent group-oriented* contingencies mean that each member of the group must achieve a specified level of performance in order for the group to get the reward. An example would be the entire class earning one period of free time if everyone passes the science test by with at least 80%.

Other Strategies for Behavior Management

- Counseling Techniques—include life-space interview, reality therapy, and active listening.

- Consequences should be as close as possible to the outside world, especially for adolescents.

- Students, especially older students, should participate as much as possible in the planning, goal-setting, and evaluation of their behavior management plans.

- Because adolescents frequently have a number of reinforcers outside of school, the teacher should try to incorporate contingencies for school behavior at home, since parents can control important reinforcers such as movies, going out with friends, car privileges, etc.

- Consistency, especially with adolescents, reduces the occurrence of power struggles and teaches them that predictable consequences follow for their choice of actions.

- Initially, the target behavior may increase or worsen when the student realizes that the behavior no longer is reinforced. However, if the behavior management plan is properly administered, the teacher should begin to see results. Behavior management plan evaluation is a continuous process, since changes in behavior require changes in the target behavior, looking for outside variables that may account for behavior change, or changes in reinforcement schedules and menus.

COMPETENCY 8.0   Deals with misconduct, interruptions, intrusions, and digressions in ways that promote instructional momentum.

Skill 8.1   Recognizes factors, in and out of school, which contribute to student misconduct.

One of the fundamental prerequisites in dealing with student misbehavior is the knowledge that all behavior is the result of something else. All teachers are trained to be aware of acceptable and unacceptable behaviors and know that when a child misbehaves, there is always a reason. Children who are developing within the normal range, are usually eager to please the adults that are important in their lives, at least until the adolescent stage. Therefore, when a child misbehaves, the teacher needs to be mindful of the contributing factors before addressing the behavior with the child or the child's parents.

The teacher who knows his/her class well and is "withit" will be cognizant of what is happening in every corner of the classroom between and among the children at all times. It should be relatively easy to identify problems that occur during the school day since the teacher observes the students as they interact with one another. Should the teacher be unaware of problems between students, misbehavior will surely occur. At this point in time the teacher will then tune in to the child who is misbehaving and hopefully, will soon be able to see what is happening to cause misbehaviors. As with anything else, the best way to solve behavior problems is to prevent them. The "withit" teacher frequently knows when and why problems will occur and will act to eliminate potential provocations. The simplest means of preventing conflict between students who are having a problem with one another is to give them their own space and to separate them.

It is considerably more difficult for a teacher to know what problems a child may be experiencing at home but the effective teacher knows that children only misbehave when a problem exists. Misbehavior may include lying, stealing, aggression, crying, shouting out, saying hurtful things, and being disrespectful to both other children and adults. The teacher who has been successful at establishing a rapport with the students' families will be much more effective in both preventing and desisting misbehavior. When families are comfortable with and trust the teacher, they will confide in the teacher and will likely make the teacher aware of family difficulties which may contribute to student misbehavior.

When the family chooses not to confide in the teacher or other person at the school, the teacher is still responsible for addressing misbehavior. One of the first steps in dealing with student misbehavior is to contact the parents and discuss the problem with them asking for their support. Sometimes parents are so involved with life's problems that they do not recognize that their child is also having problems. At other times, parents do realize that their child has a problem but deny the connection between the child's problem and their own problems. Nevertheless, most parents will respond to a teacher's request for support especially when they believe that the teacher truly cares about their child and wants to help the child. It is essential for the teacher to express concern rather than to be perceived as complaining or disliking a child.

Unfortunately, at times misbehavior is the result of specific teacher actions. There is considerable research that indicates that some teacher behavior is upsetting to students and increases the occurrence of student misbehavior. Such teacher behavior may include any action that a child perceives as being unfair, punitive remarks about the child, his behavior or his work, or harsh responses to the child.

Skill 8.2   Correctly identifies the students who misbehave and gives clear statements concerning the violation and the expectation without over-dwelling, expressing roughness, and creating undue emotional tension.

Children believe that their teacher has "eyes in the back of her head". The withit teacher is truly aware of what the students are doing and sends this message to the students through her behavior. When a deviancy occurs in the classroom, the effective teacher knows which student(s) has caused the deviancy and swiftly stops the behavior before the deviant conduct spreads to other students or becomes more serious. The teacher who knows how to desist a deviancy not only stops the deviancy but also has a marked positive effect upon the other students.

When the teacher attempts to desist a deviancy, what she says and how she says it directly influence the probability of stopping the misbehavior. The effective teacher demonstrates that she is aware of what the entire class is doing and is in control of the behavior of all students even when the teacher is working with only a small group of children. In an attempt to prevent student misbehaviors the teacher makes clear, concise statements about what is happening in the classroom directing attention to content and the students' accountability for their work rather than focusing the class on the misbehavior. It is also effective for the teacher to make a positive statement about the appropriate behavior that she is observing. If deviant behavior does occur, the effective teacher will specify who the deviant is, what he or she is doing wrong, and why this is unacceptable conduct or what the proper conduct would be. This can be a difficult task to accomplish as the teacher must maintain academic focus and flow while addressing and desisting misbehavior. She must make clear, brief statements about her expectations without raising her voice and without disrupting instruction.

The teacher must be careful to control her voice, both the volume and the tone. Expressions intended to stop deviant behavior that are perceived as angry or punitive may result in ending the undesirable behavior but, at the same time, will probably cause an increase in emotional tension. Research indicates that soft reprimands are more effective in controlling disruptive behavior than loud reprimands and that when soft reprimands are used fewer are needed. The findings of studies of desist techniques (Kounin and Alden, 1970) include: elementary students who witnessed a punitive or angry desist responded with more behavior disruptions; high school students who witnessed a desist with roughness not only felt discomfort but also regarded the disruption as more serious and at the same time lost focus of the lesson; when a simple reprimand was observed, students felt the teacher was fairest and able to maintain control of the class while preserving academic focus.

Skill 8.3   Attends to two tasks at the same time without affecting ongoing instruction.

The teacher who can attend to a task situation and an extraneous situation simultaneously without becoming immersed in either one is said to have "withitness". This ability is absolutely imperative for teacher effectiveness and success. It can be a difficult task to address deviant behavior while sustaining academic flow, but this is a skill that teachers need to develop early in their careers and one that will become second nature, intuitive, instinctive.

Teacher withitness is defined in the Florida Performance Measurement System Domains as, "teacher behavior that indicates to the students that the teacher knows what they are doing" at all times and at the same time can continue instruction. Withitness has been found to positively effect both classroom behavior management and student task involvement. Teachers who have been specially trained in withitness, report positive correlation's between their withitness and reading achievement as well as reductions in student misbehaviors and disruptions. Teacher training in withitness techniques includes how to implement positive questioning techniques, using alerting cues, giving goal-directed prompts, using a soft voice when making reprimands, integrating alternative behavior desists, and applying concurrent and specific praise. Research in regard to teacher withitness indicate that teachers who are comfortable with the above techniques and are "withit" increase instructional time by at least twenty minutes per day and decrease deviant behavior significantly. Further, withitness techniques have been found to apply to boys as well as girls, to emotionally disturbed children as well as non-disturbed children, and to both younger and older grade children. They also apply to the entire class as well as to individual students.

Skill 8.4   Uses appropriate verbal and/or nonverbal techniques for reinforcing and modifying student behavior.

It has already been established that appropriate verbal techniques include a soft non-threatening voice void of undue roughness, anger, or impatience regardless of whether the teacher is instructing, providing student alert or giving a behavior reprimand.

Verbal techniques which may be effective in modifying student behavior include simply stating the student's name, explaining briefly and succinctly what the student is doing that is inappropriate and what the student should be doing. Verbal techniques for reinforcing behavior include both encouragement and praise delivered by the teacher. In addition, for verbal techniques to positively effect student behavior and learning, the teacher must give clear, concise directives while implying her warmth toward the students.

Other factors which contribute to enhanced student learning have to do with body language. The teacher needs to make eye contact with individual students, smile and nod approvingly, move closer to the students, give gentle pats on the shoulder, arm or head, and bend over so that the teacher is face to face with the children. Some of these same techniques can be applied as a means of desisting student misbehaviors. Rather than smiling, the teacher may need to make eye contact first and then nod disapprovingly. Again a gentle tap on the shoulder or arm can be used to get a student's attention in an attempt to stop deviancy.

It is also helpful for the teacher to display prominently the classroom rules. This will serve as a visual reminder of the students' expected behaviors. In a study of classroom management procedures, it was established that the combination of conspicuously displayed rules, frequent verbal references to the rules, and appropriate consequences for appropriate behaviors led to increased levels of on-task behavior.

Skill 8.5   Identifies and uses parental assistance and/or school and community resources to modify student behavior.

When the teacher is unable to modify student behavior using all the appropriate verbal and nonverbal techniques, she must seek the support and assistance of the parents. One of the first steps in dealing more effectively with students is to establish a rapport with the student's parents. The second step is to communicate regularly with the student's parents being sure to report positive occurrences as well as any problems which may develop. A common procedure in modifying deviant behavior is to initiate a daily report. This is a written two-way communication between the school and the family and is usually a simple checklist of behaviors that occurred that day. The parents sign the report and return it along with any questions or comments to the teacher the following day. The daily report system includes consequences for misbehaviors and rewards for appropriate behavior which are delivered by the parents.

In the rare instances when neither the teacher nor the parents are able to modify student deviant behavior, a third party is contacted. Often this third party is a community resource program. It is the responsibility of the teacher to be familiar with such programs in order to help in meeting the needs of students. These agencies are equipped to address serious behavioral problems such as emotional disorders, psychological problems, and other disruptive disorders. These programs involve family counseling as well as individual counseling and sometimes they even offer parenting classes.

FLORIDA TEACHER CERTIFICATION EXAM

ADDITIONAL INFORMATION REGARDING PROFICIENCY IN BEHAVIOR MANAGEMENT

Skill : Identify and explain assertive discipline.

Assertive discipline, developed by Canter and Canter, is an approach to classroom control that allows the teacher to constructively deal with misbehavior and maintain a supportive environment for the students. The assumptions behind assertive discipline are:

- Behavior is a choice
- Consequences for not following rules are natural and logical, not a series of threats or punishments.
- Positive reinforcement occurs for desired behavior
- The focus is on the behavior and the situation, not the students character

The assertive discipline plan should be developed as soon as the teacher meets the students. The students can become involved in developing and discussing the needs for the rules. Rules should be limited to 4 to 6 basic classroom rules which are simple to remember and positively stated (e.g., Raise hand to speak instead of Don' talk without permission

1. Recognize and remove roadblocks to assertive discipline. Replace negative expectations with positives, and set reasonable limits for the children.

2. Practice an assertive response style. That is, clearly state teacher expectations and expect the students to comply with them.

3. Set limits. Take into consideration the students behavioral needs, the teachers expectations, and set limits for behavior. Decide what you will do when the rules are broken or complied with.

4. Follow through promptly with the consequences when students break the rules. However, the students should clearly know in advance what to expect when a rule is broken. Conversely, also follow through with the promised rewards for compliance and good behavior. This reinforces the concept that individuals choose their behavior and that there are consequences for their behavior.

5. Devise a system of positive consequences. Positive consequences do not have to always be food or treats. However, rewards should not be promised if it is not possible to deliver them. The result is a more positive classroom.

Skill : Identify and explain teacher effectiveness training.

The concept behind Gordon's Teacher Effectiveness Training lies in Carl Roger's assumption that each person is unique and views and experiences the world in a different way. Therefore, people should not make decisions for others because their point of view and experiences are not the same. (A more detailed explanation may be found in Wolfgang and Glickman.)

T.. E. T. addresses the basic need for students to conform to classroom rules and the teacher to maintain order. According to T. E. T., teachers get students to conform to the classroom rules in one of three ways:

Noninterventionist—Students are given the power to control their own behavior. This does not mean that the teacher does not directly intervene in situations where the student's behavior is detrimental to self or others.

Interventionist—The teacher controls the power over students' behavior and gradually allows the students to assume more and more control as they demonstrate their ability to control their behavior.

Shared Power—The teacher and students share the power of control. Depending on the student's behavior, the teacher may decide to use either an interventionist or noninterventionist approach. In T.E.T., the classroom is viewed as a supportive model, where teachers and students share power.

When a problem or conflict occurs, first step in T.E.T. is to decide ownership of the problem. There are three possibilities—

A. The student owns the problem when the behavior has no concrete effect on anyone else. An example would be a Stacey feeling rejected because a boy she really liked invited someone else to the prom. Since no one else feels rejected, it is that student's problem.

B. No problem—the behavior is not negatively affecting anyone, including the student. An example would be a student quietly playing a computer game during free time.

C. The teacher owns the problem—The students behavior is having a concrete effect on the teacher. An example would be a student interjecting wisecracks during a lecture. The teacher has a problem because he cannot achieve his objective of carrying out the lecture effectively.

When the problem belongs to the student, the teacher can choose a response from a continuum that ranges from visually looking on to physical intervention. The steps are summarized here:

1. Visually Looking On. In the case of Stacey, she may respond to the loss of a point on the point sheet with an angry outburst about how no one likes her, including the teacher.

The teacher's response at this stage would be to listen critically to what the student is saying and acknowledge his or her feelings.

2. Nondirective statements. The teacher shows that he or she listened to the student by using the active listening technique of mirroring. A response might be, You seem to feel that everyone is rejecting you.

(If the problem was a teacher-owned problem, the teacher would use an I message, that describes the behavior and the effect that it is having on the teacher. An example would be, When you get angry and throw books, I am afraid that another student or I might get hurt. This way, the problem is returned to the student.)

3. Questions. When the teacher has acknowledged the student's feelings, the next step is the use of door openers or questions that invite the student to talk about what triggered the outburst. Such statements as Do you want to talk about it? are non-judgmental and supportive. Through further discussion and problem-solving techniques, the student and teacher can arrive at a resolution.

4. Directive statements. When used correctly, Gordon calls directive statements influencing attempts. Such conditions are those where the teacher must use a strong direction, order, or command to prevent a student from endangering himself or others. However, Gordon warns teachers that they may inadvertently create conflict through the overuse of directive statements. Overused, directive statements become roadblocks to the student-teacher relationship. Categories of directive statements which may be overused include:

- Ordering, commanding, directing
- Warning, threatening
- Moralizing, preaching, and should and ought to statements
- Offering advice, solutions, and suggestions
- Lecturing and giving logical arguments

These types of statements, according to T.E.T., are not effective because they represent the teachers solution to the students problem. Other types of roadblock statements are put-downs, judgments, and evaluations:

- Judging, criticizing, blaming, disagreeing
- Name-calling, stereotyping labeling
- Interpreting, analyzing, diagnosing
- Praising, agreeing, and giving positive evaluation (in order to influence a student's behavior)
- Reassuring, sympathizing, consoling, supporting

Gordon notes that the last two types of roadblocks in the previous examples are strong reinforcement techniques of many behavior management systems. In order to understand this apparent contradiction, it is necessary to consider these in the context of Gordon's view of the use of authority. Type I authority is based on a persons expertise, knowledge, and experiences. This is desirable authority. On the other hand, Type II authority is undesirable because the teacher's authority is based on the ability to use rewards and punishments as a tool to change behavior. Gordon views these as a misuse of power that produces defensive actions by students such as:

rebelling	lying	cheating	withdrawing
tattling	bullying	conforming`	submission
regressing	needing to win,	hating to lose	apple polishing

The T.E.T. teacher sees such behavior as a signal to change his or her behavior back to Type I authority. The effective teacher used modeling through no lose conflict resolution and modeling through daily actions to influence students behavior. Reinforcement in T.E.T. is done me, individually, or optimum time for working with the teacher). When all other methods have not worked, then the teacher may need to use physical intervention and isolation with the student. Physical intervention and isolation must be done in a manner that respects the dignity of the student, is safe, and is in a time consistent with the age of the child.

Identify and explain the philosophy or characteristics of behavior modification.

Behavior modification is a model of behavior change based on the findings of B. F. Skinner called operant conditioning.. Antecedent and consequences are systematically applied for the purpose of strengthening, maintaining, or weakening an operant behavior. Operant behavior is controlled by the central nervous system and voluntary muscles, unlike Pavlov's respondent conditioning, where behaviors are controlled by involuntary muscles. Operant behaviors usually occur first, and then are modified by the resulting stimulus event (consequent stimulus event, or CSE). For example, if you hit a person (the operant behavior) and that person hits back (the CSE), your hitting behavior will probably be weakened. If you exercise (operant behaviors) and lose 5 pounds (the CSE), your exercise behavior will probably be strengthened.

Operant behaviors can be influenced by environmental events that precede them. These events are referred to as antecedent stimulus event (ASE). An example would be a teacher asking a student a question (ASE). The student's answer would be the operant behavior, which, in turn, would be weakened. maintained, or strengthened by the teacher's reaction (CSE) to the response.

CSE are called reinforcers when they strengthen an operant behavior. Reinforcement may be positive (R+) or negative (R-). Positive reinforcement occurs when an operant behavior is immediately followed with a reward or something desirable to that person. An example would be a child receiving a sticker for a correct spelling test. The prospect of receiving another sticker will probably strengthen the child's incentive to continue to study for spelling tests. Negative reinforcement occurs when an operant behavior is strengthened because the behavior is immediately followed with the removal or avoidance of something unpleasant. An example would be obeying the speed limit on I-95 because we want to avoid getting stopped by a police car and having to pay an expensive traffic ticket. The negative reinforcement of avoiding traffic tickets strengthens the likelihood of the driver continuing to obey the speed limit.

Extinction is the weakening of an operant behavior by withholding a known positive reinforcer. An example would be a teacher ignoring students if they call out without raising their hands. If student Joe calls out without raising his hand and the teacher ignores him, Joe will probably stop calling out and raise his hand to be recognized.

Punishment occurs when an operant behavior is followed with an unpleasant or aversive CSE. Punishment is often confused with negative reinforcement. It should be remembered that punishment weakens an operant behavior by presenting an aversive consequence while negative reinforcement strengthens an operant behavior by removing the aversive consequence. A CSE is not a true punisher unless it weakens the behavior. An example of punishment is a student losing a point on her point sheet for talking out. If the student does not care about the daily point sheet in the first place and continues to talk, losing the point is not an effective punisher.

Reinforcers and punishers are grouped in two classes:

A.   Unlearned (primary or unconditioned) do not have to be paired with other reinforcers or punishers for learning to take place   Food and pain are examples of unlearned reinforcers and punishers.

B.   Learned (secondary or conditioned) reinforcers and punishers must be paired with an unlearned reinforcer or punisher to become effective. An example would be a mother smiling as she gives her baby his bottle or food. The baby would then learn to associate smiles with good things. In Pavlov's classic experiment, a bell was rung when food was presented to dogs, who salivated at the prospect of being fed. Eventually, the dogs began to associate the bell with mealtime, and salivated at the sound even when no food was presented.

Reciprocal Relationships refer to the conditioning of one's behavior as a result of his or her attempts to modify another person's behavior through reinforcers, punishment, or extinction. An example would be a child who throws a tantrum when she does not get what she wants and the parent gives in to stop the tantrum. The child's tantrum behavior was strengthened by getting what she wanted; the parent's behavior was modified because he learned that giving the child her way was a means to avoid noisy tantrums.

Skill : Identify and explain values clarification.

Values clarification (Raths and Simon) is a method of helping students explore their attitudes, aspirations, purposes, and behaviors through a process that enables them to choose a future course of action from alternatives. (For a more detailed explanation, refer to Wolfgang and Glickman.) As defined by Raths, Harmin, and Simon, a value is the outcome of a three part process which has seven characteristics. Statements of belief which are not the result of this process are not considered true values. (Wolfgang and Glickman, p. 64)

Choosing

1. freely
2. from alternatives
3. after thoughtful consideration of the consequences of each alternative

Prizing:

4. cherishing, being happy with the choice
5. willing to affirm the choice publicly

Acting

6. doing something with the choice
7. repeatedly, in some pattern of life

In a values clarification lesson, the teacher presents a role-play situation to the group. There is no ending—the teacher asks the students to think and then write down their answer about what they would do if they were in the situation. The students could then take turns role-playing their actions, suggest alternative ways to the situation, and explain their choices.

According to Rath, much of a students misbehavior results from not knowing or thinking about his or her values. There are three reasons for a student's misbehavior:

mental or physical abilities—The student uses his brains or physical abilities to get what he wants, even if it negatively impacts others. An example would be Joey may persuade Josh to give him the basketball because Josh is afraid that Joey will hit him.

emotional experiences—The student may act out of emotional trauma or fears associated with previous experiences. For instance, Shelley, a fourth grader, may deliberately talk and interrupt the teacher in order to get sent out of math class. Math is her poorest subject, and some of the students have laughed at her and called her stupid.

lack of values—The student misbehaves because he or she has no inner standards to suggest that the behavior is wrong. Marcus never says "I'm sorry." or "Excuse me" when he needs to interrupt a conversation or accidentally bumps into someone. In his household, family members interrupt when they want to say something and never say

"Excuse me" at all.

The teachers role in the values clarification process is to guide students to internalize the desired code of behavior through their own ability to freely examine, analyze, and choose to accept that value. The teacher must remain nonjudgmental and set up situations, informal and formal, that give the student the chance to examine his or her present values about a situation, analyze and generate alternatives, and make future choices about that value.

Values clarification is not designed to deal with immediate instances of disruptive behavior. Because values are acquired and changed gradually, the technique is part of a long-term intervention plan for helping students develop value and decision-making skills. Values clarification also requires sufficient time to implement because students (especially students with behavior problems) often need many opportunities to practice the process of self-examination, evaluating, and choosing.

In values clarification, the opportunity to examine values is not confined to structured lessons. The daily classroom setting can give the teacher occasion to use active listening to identify the students values through their spontaneous statements. Statements that reflect a students attitudes, aspirations, purposes, interests, or activities are called indicators. However, the teacher must keep in mind that a true value conforms to the seven criteria listed above.

The teachers most important tool in values clarification is questioning. After listening to what the student says and making nondirected, nonjudgemental statements that invite the student to continue, the teacher can ask questions to see if the statement is a true value. The teacher must be careful not to use questions that are actually directed statements such as "Do you believe that is the way a person should act?" Such types of questions are actually value influences.

Examples of values clarification exercises are those that ask the students to rank, sort, order, complete open-ended sentences, role play, and interviews. No student should be forced to participate. The authors (see Wolfgang and Glickman, p. 65) recommend the techniques for students who are

- apathetic
- flighty
- uncertain
- inconsistent
- drifters
- overconformers
- overdissenters
- role players

Skill : Identify and explain the psychoeducational techniques.

The psychoeducational model is a general strategy for the education and management of children. The model (Long, Morse, and Newman, 1976) incorporates psychoanalytical and educational techniques for children with behavioral problems.

1.   The pupil should be described in terms of functioning skills that emphasizes strengths and points out weaknesses for remediation.

2.   In the psychoeducational model, the classroom is a specialized environment where the child can function successfully at his or her present level and where the student is taught that he or she is capable of functioning appropriately.

3.   The adults should understand how each pupil feels, perceives, thinks, and behaves in this setting in order to help the student change. Throughout the day there will be opportunities to learn how to change maladaptive behavior.

4.   The teachers are responsible for being aware of the areas where their students are vulnerable in normal tasks and relationships and adjust their own behavior accordingly. They should listen to what the pupil is saying, and initially expect and accept a normal amount of hostility and disappointment from students and colleagues.

5.   Emotionally disturbed children will behave in aggressive or immature ways when they are under stress. They can spread their feelings in other children. When that child is successful in getting other children to recreate these feelings (i.e., hyperactivity, aggression, withdrawal), this reinforces the child's resistance to changing his or her behavior. Adults must act in a mature fashion even though it may be difficult at times.

6.   Emotionally disturbed children often associate adult interventions with rejection. The adults must continually reassure the pupil that they are there to protect him or her. The teachers personal appearance, attitudes, and behaviors can all serve to reinforce this reassurance.

7.   Crisis are excellent opportunities for teaching and learning. Behavioral limits can be a form of love, and physical restraint can be a therapeutic act of caring for children.

8.   Teachers must demonstrate fairness in dealing with children. While there should be group rules, there should also be individualized expectations to help children develop and change their maladaptive behavior.

9.   Students should learn social and academic skills to strengthen their capacity to cope with stress in their environment. When there are problems in the students home or community life, the school can become an important source of support for the students.

Skill : Identify and explain systematic physical intervention.

Systemic physical intervention refers to removal of students when they are out of control and their classmates attention is drawn to the behavior. For less severe infractions, the student may be placed in exclusion time-out, where he or she can observe the rest of the class, but does not receive any reinforcement. Exclusion time-out is for a short time, usually 5 to 15 minutes, depending on the age of the child and severity of the misbehavior. After the set time, the student rejoins the class and has the opportunity to receive reinforcement and participate in the class activities. Seclusion time-out means removal to a special area such as a time-out room, where the student receives no verbal or social reinforcement for a designated period of time.

Systemic physical intervention is part of a continuum of interventions and teacher behaviors in response to student misbehavior. It is an effective intervention for highly disruptive or aggressive behavior if it is properly used. Guidelines for physical intervention include:

1.   Physical intervention should be included as part of a total behavior management plan. Everyone involved in the application of the plan, including the students, should know where and when physical intervention will be used.
2.   Physical intervention should not be used when positive procedures (i.e., simple corrections or positive reinforcement) or less restrictive procedures (i.e., response cost) could be used first.
3.   Staff members should not struggle with a student in order to force him or her to enter or remain in the time out. If a student refuses to comply with time-out, then additional time or a withdrawal of a privilege should be ready to be enforced.
4.   Provide the opportunity for a student to voluntarily request placement in time-out as part of an individual behavior management plan.
5.   Periodically review the use of systemic physical intervention in the class. If the same student is being placed into time-out regularly, then the teacher must examine the situation for possible reasons. For example, withdrawn students may welcome the opportunity to go to time-out in order to avoid unpleasant situations or stressful interactions with others. By examining the environmental factors preceding a time-out, the teacher can choose methods that will reduce the need for physical intervention.

PHYSICAL INTERVENTION DURING CRISIS MANAGEMENT

Physical intervention is also used in crisis management situations where the student presents a danger to himself and/or others. Physical interventions in dangerous situations are not considered behavior management techniques, but emergency measures to keep the student safe. Programs such as Crisis Prevention and Intervention (CPI) and Benign Physical Assistance (BPA) train personnel in safe methods of transporting students to designated time-out areas. The emphasis is on preserving the safety of the students and others while maintaining respect and dignity of the individual in crisis. In such programs, physical assistance is part of a total plan, with the emphasis on early interventions before the student becomes out of control.   Again, physical intervention is practiced by trained personnel as part of a systematic plan. Interventions should not place the student in extreme discomfort or injure him. Finally, at the end of the crisis, the student should have a cool-down and debriefing with the crisis teacher or class teacher before resuming the regular program.

Skill : Identify and explain reality therapy.

Reality therapy is attributed to Glasser (1965). Its purpose is to help the student learn to face reality and behave responsibly. Each individual is assumed to be responsible for his own behavior. Inappropriate behavior is not excused on the basis of unconscious motivations.

After an episode of inappropriate behavior, the teacher interviews the student using a three-step format. The teachers role is to provide support, make no judgments about the behavior, and help the student to develop a plan to change the behavior and handle problems. The student is encouraged to realize the consequences of the behavior and make a commitment to change it.

The steps are:

1.   Help the student identify the problem by asking questions about what the student was doing at the time. For instance, if the teacher observed Mark spitting water on his classmates during water break, he might say "Mark, what were you doing in the line at the water fountain?" Through questioning, Mark will probably admit that he did indeed spit water at the fountain.

2.   Help the student develop a value judgment about the behavior by asking questions such as " Is this behavior against the rules?" or "Is this behavior helping you?"

3.   Guide the student to develop a plan to change the behavior and try to get the student to commit to the plan. Ask questions that challenge the student to think of what he or she can do to prevent the problem from reoccurring.

Skill : Identify active listening as a management technique

Active listening incorporates behaviors that the listener uses to indicate his or her interest and concern for the message the speaker is trying to communicate. Components of active listening are:

Maintaining eye contact with the speaker
Body language—learning forward and tracking the speaker
Devoting attention to the speaker and ignoring distractions
Summarizing and restating the other persons concerns

Active listening is an important part of behavior management for several reasons. By actively listening to what students are saying (or not saying), the teacher can find out what may really be bothering a student. Since many students in exceptional programs have difficulty identifying and expressing their feelings, summarization and restatement by the teacher lets the student know that the teacher understood the message. Summarization and restatement by the teacher also serves as a language model for the student. Finally, active listening serves as a way for the teacher to build a bond of support and trust by letting the student know that the teacher cares about what he or she thinks and feels.

Skill : Identify and explain stress management.

A large number of children with behavior problems also have problems coping with the problems and stresses of daily living. In many instances their living situations are quite stressful and they have either not been taught coping skills or have been expected to assume more responsibilities than they are ready for. The philosophy of stress management is that a person who learns how to cope with stress will also become more self-reliant and confident. The result is a person who feels that he or she is in control, is less likely to place the locus of control on others, and more likely to assume responsibility for his or her behavior.

Basic concepts of stress management are:

1)   Stress occurs naturally in life. A stressor is an event that usually leads to stress. Stress is the body's physiological response to that event (stressor).

2)   All stress is not bad. Eustress is the stress we feel after good excitement, such as winning the lottery. Distress, however, is a negative or disabling form of stress experienced after a frightening, dangerous, or threatening situation.

3)   The body's stress response to threats and dangers is called the General Adaptation Syndrome (G. A. S.). This is often known as "Fight or flight", and is a survival mechanism passed down from the days of early man. In the early stages of this response, the body undergoes several automatic physiological changes such as muscles tensing, increased heartbeat to pump more oxygen to the muscles, dry throat and nasal passages to let in more oxygen, and dilated pupils. Even though people today rarely need "Fight or flight"", perceived threats can begin this response. Students can learn to control this response through stress management skills, so that it does not disable or negatively influence their behavior.

4)   Stress cannot always be avoided by escaping. Getting away from one source of stress (i.e., school rules or a particular teacher) just means that another stressor will take its place.

5)   Students must learn a variety of strategies that they can use to modify their feelings, their actions, and their thoughts. They should work on one stressor at a time, usually the one easiest to correct.

6)   As a first step in learning stress coping skills, students can identify the stressors in their lives and assign a value from 1 (calm) to 10 (very distressed) to these stressors. One way to develop this awareness is by keeping a log. Through reviewing and analyzing its contents, students can learn to become aware of potentially stressful situations, as well as discriminate between major and minor stressors.

Stress Coping Skills

Students can learn to control and alleviate stress physically as well as mentally. Somatic and physiological techniques utilize controlled breathing and relaxation of muscles. Stress can also be attacked by restructuring attitudes and beliefs that lead to and reinforce stress.

A. Somatic-Physiological Skills

1)   Diaphragm breathing. This is controlled deep breathing while one concentrates on the levels of stress and using this breathing to relax and reduce stress.

2)   Progressive Relaxation Training (PRT). Through guided relaxation exercises and training, students alternately relax and tense their muscles in order to recognize what the states of tension feel like. Through training, students should eventually be able to relax all of their muscles to induce an overall and longer-lasting state of relaxation.

3)   Exercise. Aerobic exercises, including skating, cycling, jogging, and fast walking can be done in and out of school. Such exercise produces natural relaxes as well as more physically fit.

B. Cognitive-Psychological Coping Skills

1.   Ellis ' ABC model and cognitively mediated stress. In this model, events (A) do not cause the stress ©. Our beliefs (B) and what we say to ourselves produce the stress. These beliefs make the difference between a rational fear (a growling pit bull dog) and an irrational fear (fear of all dogs whether they are angry or not), or a mildly unpleasant situation (getting turned down for a date) and the of the world (no one is ever going to date me because I must be a jerk.)

2.   Problem Solving. The basic problem solving steps involve: (a) Identify the problem, (b) Consider the choices. © For each choice, ask questions, such as Will this hurt me or others? ,What are the consequences of this choice?, What are the pros and cons of this choice?, (d) Choose a solution and do it. (e) Evaluate the effectiveness of the solution, and (f) If the solution was not effective, select an alternative.

        Stress Inoculation. This strategy incorporates a variety of skills and targets anxiety and anger. Phase 1 consists of teaching basic concepts about stress and stress management. Phase 2 involves relaxation training. Phase 3 focuses on cognitive restructuring of irrational beliefs contributing to the high levels of anxiety or anger. Phase 4 is the stress script stage, where the students writes the things he or she needs to say or do before, during, and after an encounter with the stressful situation. Role playing and rehearsal provide practice using the script. Phase 5 is the inoculation state where the student uses the stress script during an actual stressful situation. Positive self-talk is important after the encounter, where the student analyzes the success of the stress script and looks for areas of possible improvement.

Skill : Identify environmental influences on behavior.

Behavior does not occur in a vacuum. It occurs in a variety of settings, with a variety of people, and in a variety of situations. Thus, behavior change must also take into consideration the environmental influences that may influence or maintain a students problem behavior.

Step 1 in assessing the environment is to precisely identify the target behavior. Use the 5 W (who, what, where, when, and why) questions to clearly define the behavior problem.

Step 2 involves observing the behavior in a number of settings-i.e., classroom, library, playground, cafeteria. These observations serve to identify where the behavior is causing problems, what interventions may already are being used, and also to rule out interventions which may not be effective for the setting.

Step 3 involves an analysis of the environmental reinforcers that serve to maintain or precipitate the behavior. An analysis includes information from several areas:

... The child's own ability to perceive, understand, and perform the expectations others demand. Sensory skills, developmental, and cognitive abilities all play a part in the child's ability to fit in with the environment.

... The teacher is an important part of the students environment. Things such as personality conflicts, inadvertent reinforcement of the problem behavior, lack of experience with a variety of behavior management skills, or style may be causing the behavior.

... Peer relationships are especially important in reinforcing both appropriate and inappropriate student behavior.

... Physical factors include light, noise, traffic patterns, and temperature. In the classroom desk and grouping arrangements, proximity to certain students, or distance from the blackboard all have a potential impact on behavior.

... Curriculum factors involve the ability of the child to perform the academic tasks. The child should be cognitively and developmentally able to understand the material. The teacher needs to know if the child understands and has the necessary background skills to perform the tasks as well. Finally, motivation to learn the material will more likely be higher if the teacher establishes a connection between the material and its relevance to real life situations.

... Schedules. Students vary in their levels of energy and motivation throughout the day. Certain behavior problems may result from the arrangement of activities in the daily schedule i.e., math at the end of the day or just before lunch. For older students with special needs, the difficulty of the courses should be considered before placing students in certain courses.

... Outside the school environmental influences include the family, the neighborhood, and the community. The family's values toward education, problem solving, and relationships with others heavily influences the child's attitudes in the classroom. Neighborhood influences could involve peer relationships outside the classroom, membership in gangs, church membership, and other influences of positive on negative behaviors.

Skill : Identify social/behavioral patterns from data.

Single subject research designs are useful for identifying social or behavioral patterns because the educator can control for the effects of extraneous variables and manipulate the intervention variables. This type of research design may be more effective than data-based designs, which can show patterns but do not indicate what accounts for the patterns.

Single subject research generally is done with one of these designs--:

A. Reversal Design

Also called ABAB design, data collection begins with 3 to 5 days of preintervention data to establish a baseline (A). Next comes the first intervention phase (B1), during which data is collected while the intervention is applied. To determine if the intervention was the variable that created the effect, the intervention is withdrawn to create a new baseline (A2). Finally, the intervention is applied again (B2). If the intervention was the factor that influenced the behavior, then you should see the behavior approach the initial baseline level during the time that the new intervention is withdrawn. During the second intervention period, when the intervention is reapplied, the behavior should change again.

An example of ABAB design would be using token rewards for turning in homework. A1 would be data on homework turned in with no reward. B1 would be homework assignments turned in after implementing a token reward system (hopefully the number would increase as the student proceeded through the phase). A2 would be the number of homework assignments turned in after withdrawing the token system (which would probably decrease). B2 would be the number of assignments turned in after reinstating the token system (which would probably again increase).

Reversal designs are not recommended for behaviors which would not be desirable to reinstate (like hitting or head banging). ABAB designs are also not suitable for behaviors which, once learned, would not revert to baseline levels even if the intervention were to be withdrawn (i.e., typing or swimming). In some instances, removing an intervention like praise may not be desirable.

B. Multiple Baseline Design

Multiple baseline designs are flexible in that they may be used with (a) one behavior and different students (i.e., call-outs), (b) one student and different behaviors (i.e., leaving seat and calling out), or © one student and one behavior across settings or conditions (i.e., hitting in the classroom, lunch room, and playground. Multiple baselines refer to the baselines with the different students or behaviors, not a return to the original baseline condition. Interventions may be applied to one student at a time while continuing to collect baseline data on the others, or may be applied to one behavior or setting while baseline data is collected on the other behavior. In order for this design to produce effective data, the target behaviors must be able to be separately altered without changing the rate of the other target behavior still in baseline. For example, tapping a pencil and calling out in class could probably be isolated without one affecting the other behavior. However, teasing and hitting might be interrelated and, therefore, unsuitable for this type of design.

C. Change in Criterion Design

This design is like multiple baseline, except it is intended to be used with only one student, behavior, and setting. After collecting data for the original baseline, the intervention is applied through gradually increasing criterion levels. If the behavior continues to meet the increases in expectations, then it may be concluded that the intervention was responsible for the changes. An example of this design would be amount of time spent on task for a child who is frequently off-task. After collecting baseline data, the teacher would implement the intervention (i.e., using a timer) while the expected level of performance (in this case, amount of time spent on task) gradually increases.

D. Data-based interventions

This design involves collecting data on a students academic or behavioral performance towards a goal. Baseline periods usually are from 3 to 5 days, but may be extended if the data are variable or a therapeutic trend is apparent. During the program implementation data is collected. In order to identify the trend, a line is drawn through the line of best fit which connects as much of the points as possible. Another method of determining a trend line is to divide the data in half, calculate the median or mean of each group, and connecting those points.

In interpreting the effectiveness of the program, look at the baseline trend and the program trend line. If the goal of the baseline trend is in the direction of the program goal, it might be difficult to attribute the change to the program, since the behavior is changing anyway. If the baseline trend is stable or in a direction opposite to the goal, then desirable changes in the trend after program implementation could be attributed to the effectiveness of the program. Unexpected extremes in the data may be due to an extraneous variable, which this type of design does not identify.

In data trend analysis, a trend line can be drawn from the baseline to the desired goal criterion. If the students performance does not meet or exceed this line of desired progress, then this indicates that changes in the program are needed. In the data decision rule, the program should be changed if the criterion is not met in any two consecutive days.

Skill : Identify social/behavioral patterns from systematic observations.

Reliability is a major issue with systematic observation. Direct measures of behavior must be appropriate for the type of behavior being observed. Data must be collected in an accurate, consistent, and systemic manner. The behavior being recorded must first be defined in specific terms so that the observer does not misinterpret or confuse the behavior. The observation period should be long enough to collect sufficient data for analysis.

1. Issues of reliability also include observer drift, a change in observer definition of the target behavior. Interrater reliability and reliability checks are a way to prevent this problem.

2. Examine what type of recording procedure was used. Permanent products such as worksheets may be interpreted in number of correct response, percents, or trials to criterion.

3. Behaviors that cannot be measured with permanent products may be recorded as Events (number of times a student called out in a half-hour period).

Duration recording is interpreted by the length of time a behavior lasted, such as amount of time a student stays out of his or her seat. This could be total duration, or duration per occurrence, which is more descriptive and useful.

Interval recording can be done with discrete (discernible beginning and end) or continuous behaviors. Interval recording can be used with one student and several behaviors or with several students observed for one behavior. The frequency of the behavior is calculated by:

Number of intervals in which the behavior occurred   X 100

Total number of intervals

In interval recording, sample intervals are short, usually about 10 to 30 seconds.

In time sampling, the intervals are longer, less frequent, and more variable. A sample could be 10 minutes every hour or 1 minute every 10 minutes. Variable intervals are useful for measuring behavior of a group relative to a rule, for example, being in seat or on task. The variable time schedule means that students cannot predict when the timer is going to signal an observation.

Interpretations can be summarized on a summary sheet, or graphed and charted. Summaries should include the dates, sessions, observation times, data taken, and the program phases or adjustments. Graphs and charts have the advantage of not only organizing the data, but are usually easy to interpret and display trends.

Data may be represented visually in several ways—

Progress chart: Bar graphs can be used for individual students or groups because they can show progress toward a goal and can be reinforcing as students fill them in.

Cumulative graphs may be used to depict rates, frequencies, percentages, time, or totals, such as collecting points toward a specified reward .   They can be used for behavior or academic purposes.

The frequency polygon (line graph) also can be used for frequency, rate, or percent data. Progress graphs or charts show the time it takes a student to master a set of objectives, which a performance chart displays a change on a single task or behavior.

COMPETENCY 9.0   Determines the entry level knowledge and/or skills of students for a given set of instructional objectives using diagnostic tests, teacher observations, and student records.

SKILL 9.1   Selects an appropriate method for assessing prerequisite knowledge, understandings and/or skills.

There are many ways to evaluate a child's knowledge and assess his/her learning needs. In recent years the emphasis has shifted from "mastery testing" of isolated skills to authentic assessments of what children know. Authentic assessments allow the teacher to know more precisely what each individual student knows, can do, and needs to do. Authentic assessments can work for both the student and the teacher in becoming more responsible for learning.

One of the simplest most efficient ways for the teacher to get to know his/her students is to conduct an entry survey. This is a record that provides useful background information about the students as they enter a class or school. Collecting information through an entry survey will give valuable insights into a student's background knowledge and experience. Teachers can customize entry surveys according to the type of information considered valuable. Some of the information that may be included include student's name and age, family members, health factors, special interests, strengths, needs, fears, etc., parent expectations, languages spoken in the home, what the child likes about school, etc.

At the beginning of each school term the teacher will likely feel compelled to conduct some informal evaluations in order to obtain a general awareness of his/her students. These informal evaluations should be the result of a learning activity rather than a "test" and may include classroom observations, collections of reading and writing samples, and notations about the students' cognitive abilities as demonstrated by classroom discussions and participation including the students' command of language. The value of these informal evaluations cannot be underestimated. These evaluations, if utilized effectively, will drive instruction and facilitate learning.

SKILL 9.2   Selects or constructs an appropriate evaluation instrument to assist in assessment of student learning needs.

After initial informal evaluations have been conducted and appropriate instruction follows, teachers will need to fine tune individual evaluations in order to provide optimum learning experiences. Some of the same types of evaluations can be used on an ongoing basis to determine individual learning needs as were used to determine initial general learning needs. It is somewhat more difficult to choose an appropriate evaluation instrument for elementary-aged students than for older students. Therefore, teachers must be mindful of developmentally appropriate instruments. At the same time, teachers must be cognizant of the information that they wish to attain from a specific evaluation instrument. Ultimately, these two factors - students' developmental stage and the information to be derived - will determine which type of evaluation will be most appropriate and valuable. There are few commercially-designed assessment tools which will prove to be as effective as the tool that is constructed by the teacher.

A simple-to-administer, information-rich evaluation of a child's reading strengths and weaknesses is the running reading record. "This technique for recording reading behavior is the most insightful, informative, and instructionally useful assessment procedure you can use for monitoring a child's progress in learning to read;" (Trail, 1993) The teacher uses a simple coding system to record what a child does while reading text out loud. At a later time the teacher can go back to the record and assess what the child knows about reading and what the teacher needs to address in an effort to help the student become a better reader.

If the teacher is evaluating a child's writing, it is a good idea to discourage the child from erasing his/her errors and to train the child to cross out errors with a single line so that the teacher can actually see the process that the student went through to complete a writing assignment. This writing becomes an important means of getting to know about students' writing and is an effective, valuable writing evaluation.

Mathematics skills can be evaluated informally by observing students as they work at their seats or perform at the board. Teachers can see if the students know basic computation skills, if they understand place value, or if they transpose numbers simply by watching them as they solve computation problems. Some teachers may prefer to administer some basic computation "tests" to determine a student's mathematics strengths and weaknesses. Although these "tests" are not as effective or thorough in assessing students, they are quick and easy to administer.

SKILL 9.3   Makes effective use of classroom observation techniques to assist in assessment of student learning needs.

One of the most valuable and effective assessment tools available to any teacher is the classroom observation. As instructional decision makers, teachers must base their instructional strategies upon students' needs. An astute observer of student behaviors and performance is most capable of choosing instructional strategies that will best meet the needs of the learners. Classroom observations take place within the context of the learning environment thus allowing the observer the opportunity to notice natural behaviors and performances.

Classroom observations should be sensitive and systematic in order to permit a constant awareness of student progress. One of the shortcomings of classroom observations is that they are often performed randomly and frequently are focused on those students whose behaviors are less than desirable. If the teacher establishes a focused observation process then observations become more valuable. It has been suggested that a teacher focus his/her observations on five or six students at a time for a period of one to two weeks.

In order for observations to truly be useful, teachers must record the information obtained from observations. When doing a formal behavioral observation, the teacher will write what the child is doing for a designated time period. At times the teacher will tally the occurrences of specific behaviors within a designated time period. When making focused observations that are ongoing the teacher may simply use a blank piece of paper with only the student's name and date written on it and space for the teacher to write anecdotal notes. Other teachers might write notes on post-it notes and put the notes in a student file. If it is not possible to record the information as it occurs and is observed, it is critical that it be recorded as soon as possible in order to maintain accuracy.

Sometimes it is helpful to do an observation simply to watch for frequency of a specific behavior. An observation can answer questions such as: Is the student on-task during independent work time? Is the student interacting appropriately with peers? Is the student using materials appropriately? These behaviors can be tallied on a piece of paper with the student's name and date of observation.

Classroom observations can provide the teacher with one of the most comprehensive means of knowing their students. Teachers can observe students to see how they interact with their peers, to see which activities they choose, what they like to read, and how frequently they choose to work alone. "Everything you hear a child say and see a child do is a glimpse into a mind and a source of information to 'know' from." (Trail, 1993)

SKILL 9.4 Makes appropriate use of information from student records to assist in assessment of student learning needs.

Currently the most uniform, commonly used form of student records available in Florida school systems is the Cumulative Record. This is a synthesis of information that provides an authentic professional account of a learner's progress and development in learning. Not only does the cumulative record contain a wealth of important information about the student, it is also fairly easy to maintain.

The cumulative record can be an invaluable resource in furnishing the teacher with data about an individual student's background including family situation; the student's school attendance; the student's medical history; the student's grades and standardized test scores; the student's behavioral background and more. This information may serve the teacher in getting to know the child and may also give the teacher insight into why the child exhibits certain behaviors and learning characteristics.

In their present format, the cumulative record is primarily used to signal any learning exceptionalities. In addition to standardized test scores, the cumulative record contains psychological testing results as well as intelligence and/or aptitude test scores. This information is usually only available for those students who have had reason to be screened for an exceptionality and can offer the teacher a wealth of assistance in addressing the student's needs immediately without the need for additional teacher-directed assessments.

SKILL 9.5   Interprets results obtained from diagnostic tests, teacher observations, and information from student records to assist in diagnosis of student learning needs and to guide instruction.

The information contained within student records, teacher observations and diagnostic tests are only as valuable as the teacher's ability to understand it. Although the student's cumulative record will contain this information, it is the responsibility of each teacher to read and interpret the information. Diagnostic test results are somewhat uniform and easy to interpret. They usually include a scoring guide which tells the teacher what the numbers actually mean. Teachers also need to realize that these number scores leave room for uncontrollable factor and are not the ultimate indicator of a child's ability or learning needs. Many factors influence these scores including the rapport the child had with the tester, how the child was feeling when the test was administered, and how the child regarded the value or importance of the test. Therefore, the teacher should regard these scores as a "ball park" figure.

When a teacher reads another teacher's observations, it is important to keep in mind that each person brings to an observation certain biases. The reader may also influence the information contained within an observation with his/her own interpretation. When using teacher observations as a basis for designing learning programs, it is necessary to be aware of these shortcomings.

Student records may provide the most assistance in guiding instruction. These records contain information that was gathered over a period of time and may show student growth and progress. They also contain information provided by several people including teachers, parents, and other educational professionals. By reading this compilation of information the teacher may get a more accurate "feel for" a student's needs. All of this information is only a stepping stone in determining how a child learns, what a child knows, and what a child needs to know to further his/her education.

COMPETENCY 10.0   Identifies long range goals appropriate to student needs.

Once long range goals have been identified and established, it is important to ensure that all goals and objectives are in conjunction with student ability and needs. Some objectives may be too basic for a higher level student, while others cannot be met with a student's current level of knowledge. There are many forms of evaluating student needs to ensure that all goals set are challenging yet achievable.

Teachers should check a students cumulative file, located in guidance, for reading level and prior subject area achievement. This provides a basis for goal setting but shouldn't be the only method used. Depending on the subject area, basic skills test, reading level evaluations, writing samples, and/or interest surveys can all be useful in determining if all goals are appropriate. Informal observation should always be used as well. Finally, it is important to take into consideration the students level of motivation when addressing student needs.

COMPETENCY 11.0   Constructs and sequences related short-range goals for a given subject area.

SKILL 11.1   Identifies knowledge, skills and attitudes to be attained for a subject area.

As a teacher one should be aware of the skills and information that are pertinent to the subject area. Teachers need to determine what a student should carry with them at the end of a term. One should also be aware of skills needed to complete any objective for that subject area and determine how skilled their students are at using them.

Because most goals are building blocks, all necessary underlying skills should be determined and a teacher must evaluate if the student has these abilities. i.e. To do mathematical word problems, students must have a sufficiently high enough level of reading to understand the problem. Are my students skilled readers?

SKILL 11.2 Constructs or adapts short-range objectives for identified knowledge, skills and attitudes.

Once the desired knowledge, skills and attitudes have been established, a teacher must develop short range objectives designed to help in the achievement of these outcomes. An objective is a specific learning outcome that is used to achieve long range goals. Objectives should be stated in observable terms such as to state, to demonstrate, to list, complete or solve. Objectives should be clear and concise, i.e. Students will be able to state five causes of World War II.

When given objectives by the school or county, teachers may wish to adapt them so that they can meet the needs of their student population. For example, if a high level advanced class is given the objective State five causes of World War II, a teacher may wish to adapt the objective to a higher level. State five causes of World War II and explain how they contributed to the start of the war. Subsequently objectives can be modified for a lower level as well. From a list of causes pick three that specifically caused World War II.

SKILL 11.3   Organizes and sequences short-range objectives consistent with commonly accepted principles of learning.

When organizing and sequencing objectives, remember that skills are building blocks. A taxonomy of educational objectives can be helpful to construct all organize objectives. Knowledge of material is low on a taxonomy and should be worked with early in the sequence. For example, memorizing definitions or memorizing famous quotes. Eventually, objectives should be developed to include higher level thinking such as comprehension, i.e. being able to use a definition; application, i.e. being able to apply the definition to other situations; synthesis, i.e. being able to add other information and evaluation, i.e. being able to judge the value of something.

COMPETENCY 12.0 Selects, adapts, and or develops instructional materials for a given set of instructional objectives and student learning needs.

SKILL 12.1 Selects materials based on instructional objectives and student learning needs and readiness levels.
See 12.3

SKILL 12.2 Adapts materials to assist students in mastering objectives.
See 12.3

SKILL 12.3 Determines materials to be developed based upon existing resources and student needs.

In considering suitable learning materials for the classroom, the teacher must have a thorough understanding of the state-mandated competency based curriculum. According to state requirements, certain objectives must be met in each subject taught at every designated level of instruction. It is necessary that the teacher become well acquainted with the curriculum for which he/she is assigned. The teacher must also be aware that it is unlawful to require students to study from textbooks or materials other than those approved by the state Department of Education.

Keeping in mind the state requirements concerning the objectives and materials, the teacher must determine the abilities of the incoming students assigned to his/her class or supervision. It is essential to be aware of their entry behavior—that is, their current level of achievement in the relevant areas. The next step is to take a broad overview of students who are expected to learn before they are passed on to the next grade or level of instruction. Finally, the teacher must design a course of study that will enable students to reach the necessary level of achievement, as displayed in their final assessments, or exit behaviors. Textbooks and learning materials must be chosen to fit into this context.

To determine the abilities of incoming students, it may be helpful to consult their prior academic records. Letter grades assigned at previous levels of instruction as well as scores on standardized tests may be taken into account. In addition, the teacher may choose to administer pre-tests at the beginning of the school year, and perhaps also at the initial stage of each new unit of instruction. The textbooks available for classroom use may provide suitable pre-tests, tests of student progress, and post-tests.

In selecting tests and other assessment tools, the teacher should keep in mind that different kinds of tests measure different aspects of student development. The tests included in most textbooks chosen for the classroom, and in the teacher's book that accompany them are usually achievement tests. Few of these are the type of tests intended to measure the students' inherent ability or aptitude. Teachers will find it difficult to raise student's scores on ability tests, but students scores on achievement tests may be expected to improve with proper instruction and application in the area being studied.

FLORIDA TEACHER CERTIFICATION EXAM

In addition to administering tests, the teacher may assess the readiness of students for a particular level of instruction by having them demonstrate their ability to perform some relevant task. In a class that emphasizes written composition, for example, students may be asked to submit writing samples. These may be used not only to assure the placement of the students into the proper level, but as a diagnostic tool to help them understand what aspects of their composition skills may need improvement. In the like manner, students in a speech class may be asked to make an impromptu oral presentation before beginning a new level or specific level of instruction. Others may be asked to demonstrate their psychomotor skills in a physical education class, display their computational skills in a mathematics class, and so on. Whatever the chosen task, the teacher will need to select or devise an appropriate assessment scale and interpret the results with care.

If students are informed their entry behaviors on such a scale, they will be better motivated, especially if they are able to observe their progress by some objective means at suitable intervals during the course. For this reason, it may be advisable to record the results of such assessments in the student's portfolios as well as in the teacher's records.

Teachers may also gauge student readiness by simply asking them about their previous experience or knowledge of the subject or task at hand. While their comments may not be completely reliable indicators of what they know or understand, such discussions have the advantage of providing an idea of the students' interest in what is being taught. Teachers can have little impact unless they are able to demonstrate how the material being introduced is relevant to the students' lives.

Keeping in mind what is understood about the students' abilities and interests, the teacher should design a course of study that presents units of instruction in an orderly sequence. The instruction should be planned so as to advance all students toward the next level of instruction, although exit behaviors need not be identical due to the inevitability of individual differences.

Most teachers chose to use textbooks, which are suitable to the age and developmental level of specific student populations. Textbooks reflect the values and assumptions of the society which produces them, while they also represent the knowledge and skills considered to be essential in becoming an educated adult. Finally, textbooks are useful to the school bureaucracy and the community, for they make public and accessible the private world of the classroom.

Though these factors may favor the adoption of textbooks, the individual teacher may have only limited choice about which textbooks to use, since such decisions are often made by the school administration or the local school district (In observance of the state guidelines). If teachers are consulted about textbook selection, it is likely that they have little training in evaluation techniques, and they are seldom granted leave time to encourage informed decisions. On those occasions when teachers are asked to assist in the selection process, they should ask, above all, whether the textbooks have real substance—is World War II accurately chronicled, does the science textbook correctly conceptualize electrical current, do literary selections reflect a full range of genre?

From time to time, controversy has arisen about the possible weakness of textbooks—the preponderance of pictures and illustrations, the avoidance of controversy in social studies textbooks, the lack of emphasis on problem-solving in science books, and so on. In the 1980's, certain books were criticized for their attention to the "liberal" or "secular" values, and the creationism/evolution argument has re-surfaced again and again. Finally, recent decades have witnessed a movement to grant more attention to women, Afro-Americans, and other groups whose contributions to our developing culture may have been overlooked in earlier textbooks. Individual teachers would be well advised to keep themselves informed of current trends or developments, so as to make better informed choices for their students and deal with the possibility of parental concern.

Focusing on the needs evident in almost any classroom population, the teacher will want to use textbooks that include some of the activities and selections to challenge the most advanced students as well as those who have difficulty in mastering the material at a moderate pace. Some of the exercises may be eliminated altogether for faster learners, while students who have difficulty may need to have material arranged into brief steps or sections. For almost any class, some experience in co-operative learning may be advisable. Thus the faster learners will reinforce what they have already mastered, while those of lesser ability at the tasks in question can ask about their individual problems or areas of concern. Most textbook exercises intended for independent work can be used in cooperative learning, though in most cases, teachers will encourage better participation if the cooperating group is asked to hand in a single paper or project to represent their combined efforts, rather than individual papers or projects. This method does not always require that all members of the group be assigned the same grade (If letter grades are assigned at all for such assignments). Depending on what students have been told before starting the activity, the teacher may be justified in adjusting grades accordingly if he/she observes some students applying more effort than the others to the cooperative learning endeavor.

In choosing materials, teachers should also keep in mind that not only do students learn at different rates, but they bring a variety of cognitive styles to the learning process. Prior experiences influence the individual's cognitive style, or method of accepting, processing, and retaining information. According to Marshall Rosenberg, learners can be categorized as (1)rigid-inhibited, (2)undisciplined, (3) acceptance-anxious, and (4)creative. "The creative learner is an independent thinker, one who maximizes his/her abilities, can work by his/herself, enjoys learning, and is self-critical" (1). This last category constitutes the ideal, but teachers should make every effort to use materials that will stimulate and hold the attention of learners of all types.

Aside from textbooks, there is a wide variety of materials available to today's teachers. Microcomputers are now commonplace, and some schools can now afford laser discs to bring alive the content of a reference book in text, motion, and sound. Hand-held calculators eliminate the need for drill and practice in number facts, while they also support a problem-solving and process to mathematics. Videocassettes (VCR's) are common and permit the use of home-produced or commercially produced tapes. Textbook publishers often provide films, recordings, and software to accompany the text, as well as maps, graphics, and colorful posters to help students visualize what is being taught. Teachers can usually scan the educational publishers' brochures that arrive at their principal's or department head's office on a frequent basis. Another way to stay current in the field is by attending workshops or conferences. Teachers will be enthusiastically welcomed on those occasions when educational publishers are asked to display their latest productions and revised editions of materials.

In addition, yesterday's libraries are today's media centers. Teachers can usually have opaque projectors delivered to the classroom to project print or pictorial images (including student work) onto a screen for classroom viewing. Some teachers have chosen to replace chalkboards with projectors that reproduce the print or images present on the plastic sheets known as transparencies, which the teacher can write on during a presentation or have machine-printed in advance. In either case, the transparency can easily be stored for later use. In an art or photography class, or any class in which it is helpful to display visual materials, slides can easily be projected onto a wall or a screen. Cameras are inexpensive enough to enable students to photograph and display their own work, as well as keep a record of their achievements in teacher files or student portfolios.

Studies have shown that students learn best when what is taught in lecture and textbook reading is presented more than once in various formats. In some instances, students themselves may be asked to reinforce what they have learned by completing some original production—for example, by drawing pictures to explain some scientific process, by writing a monologue or dialogue to express what some historical figure might have said on some occasion, by devising a board game to challenge the players' mathematical skills, or by acting out (and perhaps filming) episodes from a classroom reading selection. Students usually enjoy having their work displayed or presented to an audience of peers. Thus their productions may supplement and personalize the learning experiences that the teacher has planned for them.

SKILL 12.4 Designs and or selects materials based on instructional objectives,

individual student needs, and available resources.

See 12.3

SKILL 12.5 Knows and observes current copyright laws.

The advent of technology that made copying print and non-print media efficient poses serious concern for educators who unwittingly or otherwise   violate copyright law on a regular basis. Regardless of their intentions to provide their students access to materials that may be too costly for mass purchase, educators must understand the reasons for copyright protection and they must, by example, ensure the upholding of that protection.

There are many fine publications which clarify copyright law for educators. In many instances, school districts endorse these publications or provide their own concise summarizes for reference. Though all educators should be cognizant of the law, it becomes the responsibility of the school library media specialist to help inform colleagues and monitor the proper application of the law.

Actually, educators have the benefit of greater leeway in copying than any other group. Many print instructional materials carry statements that allow production of multiple copies for classroom use, provided they adhere to the "Guidelines for Classroom Copying in Nonprofit Educational Institutions." Teachers may duplicate enough copies to provide one per student per course provided that they meet the tests of brevity, spontaneity, and cumulative effect.

1. Brevity test:

   Poetry - suggested maximum 250 words.

   Prose - one complete essay, story, or article less than 2500 words <u>or</u> excerpts of no more than 1000 words or 10% of the work, whichever is less. (Children's books with text under 2500 words may not be copied in their entirety. No more than two pages containing 10% of the text may be copied.)

   Illustration - charts, drawings, cartoons, etc. are limited to one per book or periodical article.

2. Spontaneity test:

Normally copying that does not fall under the brevity test requires publisher's permission for duplication. However, allowances are made if "the inspiration and decision to use the work" occur too soon prior to classroom use for permission to be sought in writing.

3. Cumulative effect test:

Even in the case of short poems or prose, it is preferable to make only one copy. However, three short items from one work are allowable during one class term. Reuse of copied material from term to term is expressly forbidden. Compilation of works into anthologies to be used in place of purchasing texts is prohibited.

Copyright legislation has existed in the United States for more than 100 years. Conflicts over copyright were settled in the courts. The 1976 Copyright Act, especially section 107 dealing with Fair Use, created legislative criteria to follow based on judicial precedents. In 1978, when the law took effect, it set regulations for duration and scope of copyright, specified author rights, and set monetary penalties for infringement. The statutory penalty may be waived by the court for an employee of a non-profit educational institution where the employee can prove fair use intent.

Fair use, especially important to educators, is meant to create a balance between copyright protection and the needs of learners for access to protected material. Fair use is judged by the purpose of the use, the nature of the work (whether creative or informational), the quantity of the work for use, and the market effect. In essence, if a portion of a work is used to benefit the learner with no intent to deprive the author of his profits, fair use is granted.
Recently, Fair Use has been challenged most in cases of videotaping off-air of television programs. Guidelines too numerous to delineate here affect copying audio-visual materials and computer software. Most distributors place written regulations in the packaging of these products. Allowances for single back-up copies in the event of damage to the original are granted.

Section 108 is pertinent to libraries in that it permits reproducing a single copy of an entire work if no financial gain is derived, if the library is public or archival, and if the copyright notice appears on all copies.

In any event in which violation of the law is a concern, the safest course of action is to seek written permission from the publisher of the copyrighted work. If permission is granted, a copy of that permission should accompany

any duplicates.

Describe an ethically appropriate course of action regarding a violation of copyright.

When a suspected infringement of copyright is brought to the attention of the school library media specialist, she should follow certain procedures.

1. Determine if a violation has in effect occurred. Never accuse or report alleged instances to a higher authority without verification.
2. If an instance is verified, tactfully inform the violator of the specific criteria to use so that future violations can be avoided. Presented properly, the information will be accepted as constructive.
3. If advise is unheeded and further infractions occur, bring them to the attention of the teacher's supervisor - a team leader or department chair - who can handle the matter as an evaluation procedure.
4. Inform the person who has reported the alleged violation of the procedures being used.

Examine judicial rulings that have impacted library media issues.

Judicial rulings have come in the area of copyright issues. The 1975 ruling in the case of Williams & Wilkins Co. v. U.S. provided guidance to legislators in preparing the fair use provisions of the 1976 Copyright Act. It ruled that entire articles may be mass-duplicated for use which advances the public welfare without doing economic harm to the publishers. This ruling provides encouragement to educators that fair use may be interpreted more liberally.

In 1984, the ruling in the Sony Corp. of America v. Universal City Studios, Inc. placed the burden of proving infringement on the plaintiff. The Supreme Court upheld the right of individuals to off-air videotape television programs for non-commercial use. Thus, a copyright holder must prove that the use of videotaped programming is intentionally harmful. Civil suits against educators would require the plaintiff to prove that the existing or potential market would be negatively affected by use of these programs in a classroom setting.

Current fair use practice specifies that a videotaped copy must be shown within 10 days of its airing and be kept no longer than 45 days for use in constructing supplemental teaching materials related to the programming.

Court rulings have ambiguously addressed the issue of censorship. In 1972, the U.S. Court of Appeals for the Second Circuit (President's Council v.

Community School Board No. 25, New York City) ruled in favor of the removal of a library book, reasoning that its removal did not oppose or aid religion.

In 1976, the Court of Appeals for the Sixth Circuit (Minarcini v. Strongsville City School District) ruled against the removal of Joseph Heller's *Catch 22* and two Kurt Vonnequt novels on the grounds that removal of books from a school library is a burden on the freedom of classroom discussion and an infringement of the First Amendments guarantee of an individual's "right to know."

A Massachusetts district court (Right to Read Defense Committee v. School Board of the City of Chelsea) ordered the school board to return to the high school library a poetry anthology which contained "objectionable and filthy" language. The court asserted that the school had control over curriculum but not library collections.

Three cases in the 1980's dealt with challenging the removal of materials from high school libraries. The first two, in circuit courts, condemned the burning of banned books (Zykan v. Warsaw Community School Corporation, Indiana) and the removal of books of considerable literary merit. The case of Board of Education, Island Trees Union Free School District 26 (New York) v. Pico reached the Supreme Court in 1982 after the U.S. Court of Appeals for the Second Circuit had reversed a lower court ruling granting the school board the right to remove nine books which had been deemed "anti-American, anti-Semitic, anti-Christian and just plain filthy." The Supreme Court in a 5–4 ruling upheld the Court of Appeals ruling and the nine books were returned. The dissenting opinion, however, continued to foster ambiguity claiming that, if the intent was to deny free access to ideas, it was an infringement of the First Amendment, but if the intent was to remove pervasively vulgar material, the board had just cause. Ultimately, the issue hinged on a school board's authority in determining the selection of optional rather than required reading. Library books, being optional, should not be denied to users.

SKILL 12.6 Uses a variety of materials and media based upon objectives, student needs, and available resources.

See 12.3

COMPETENCY 13.0   **Selects/develops and sequences learning activities that are appropriate to instructional objectives and students needs.**

SKILL 13.1 Identifies and implements learning activities which are consistent with basic principles of human growth and development, giving consideration to various individual learning styles.

The effective teacher is cognizant of students' individual learning styles and human growth and development theory and applies these principles in the selection and implementation of appropriate instructional activities. In regards to the identification and implementation of appropriate learning activities, effective teachers select and implement instructional activities consistent with principles of human growth and development theory.

Learning activities selected for younger students (below age 8) should focus on short time frames in highly simplified form. The nature of the activity and the content in which the activity is presented effects the approach that the students will take in processing the information. Younger children tend to process information at a slower rate than older children (age 8 and older).

On the other hand, when selecting and implementing learning activities for older children, teachers should focus on more complex ideas as older students are capable of understanding more complex instructional activities. Moreover, effective teachers maintain a clear understanding of the developmental appropriateness of activities selected for providing educational instructions to students and select and present these activities in a manner consistent with the level of readiness of his/her students.

SKILL 13.2 Selects or develops activities that recognize conditions that affect learning.

The effective teacher takes care as to select appropriate activities and classroom situations in which learning is optimized. The classroom teacher should manipulate instructional activities and classroom conditions in a manner that enhances group and individual learning opportunities. For example, the classroom teacher can organize group learning activities in which students are placed in a situation in which cooperation, sharing ideas, and discussion occurs. Cooperative learning activities can assist students in learning to collaborate and share personal and cultural ideas and values in a classroom learning environment.

SKILL 13.3 Selects or develops appropriate learning activities to achieve objective(s).

The effective teacher selects learning activities based on specific learning objectives. Ideally, teachers should not plan activities which fail to augment the specific objectives of the lesson. Learning activities should be planned with a learning objective in mind. Objective driven learning activities tend to serve as a tool to reinforce the teacher's lesson presentation. Additionally, selected learning objectives should be consistent with state and district educational goals which focus on National educational goals (Goals 2000) and the specific strengths and weaknesses of individual students assigned to the teacher's class.

SKILL 13.4 Combines appropriate learning activities into an instructional sequence.

The effective teacher plans his/her learning activities as to introduce them in a meaningful instructional sequence. Teachers should combine instructional activities as to reinforce information by providing students with relevant learning experiences through instructional activities.

COMPETENCY 14.0 Uses class time efficiently.
SKILL 14.1 Begins classwork promptly.

Punctuality is defined as when a "teacher begins classwork promptly." It further states that if class is delayed for ten minutes, over the school year, almost two months of instruction is lost. Therefore, it is very important to begin class on time. Effective teachers are punctual. This is because punctuality leads to more on-task time which results in greater subject matter retention among the students.

There are a number of things that hinder teachers from beginning instruction immediately. Some examples are: attendance, discipline or just getting students to settle down. Effective teachers have pre-determined plans to deal with these distractions.

Dealing with the daily task of attendance can be done efficiently and quickly with the use of a seating chart. A teacher can spot absentees in seconds by noting the empty seats, rather than calling each student's name which could take as long as five minutes. During this laborious roll-calling time is also the ideal situation for deviant behaviors to occur, resulting in further off-task time. Therefore, the use of seating charts leads to more on-task time. Another time-saving technique is to laminate the seating chart. This allows the teacher to make daily notes right on the chart. The teacher may also efficiently keep track of who is volunteering and who is answering questions. The effective teacher uses this information to create an equitable classroom climate for all students.

Deviant behavior can lead to more off-task time than any other factor in today's classrooms. Effective teachers reduce the incidence of these behaviors through clear-cut rules and consistency. If the teacher is consistent, then the students know what to expect, and learn very quickly that they, too, must be consistent. The Professional Orientation Program teaches that effective teachers state the rules, explain the rules, and then put the students through a guided practice of the rules. This results in a clear understanding of what behaviors are expected in the classroom from each student. Moreover, it is more efficient to reduce the occurrence of deviant behaviors rather than to have to deal with them happening. Effective teachers achieve this through clear-cut rule explication and consistent monitoring.

Furthermore, effective teachers maintain a business-like atmosphere in the classroom. This leads to the students getting on-task quickly when instruction begins. There are many ways effective teachers begin instruction immediately. One method is through the use of over-head projectors. The teacher turns-on the overhead the second class begins, and the students begin taking notes. The teacher is then free to circulate for the first few minutes of class and settle-down individual students as necessary. Additionally, having a routine that is followed regularly at the beginning of class allows the students to begin without waiting for teacher instruction. Therefore, effective teachers maintain business-like consistent classrooms.

FLORIDA TEACHER CERTIFICATION EXAM

In conclusion, effective teachers utilize an efficient use of class time. The teacher understands it is important to begin class promptly because of the enormous amount of teaching time that can be lost. Therefore, effective teachers attend to attendance procedures, and other non-academic tasks routinely while maintaining on-task behavior among the students.

SKILL 14.2   Focuses teacher and student talk on academic subject matter.

Effective teachers maintain the academic focus in the classroom by controlling the discourse at all times. This is effective because when the teacher controls the verbal information the probability of student comprehension is increased. Control of discourse is achieved through what the Performance Measurement System: Domains (PMS Domains) calls connected discourse. Connected discourse is defined as "thematically connected discourse that leads to at least one point." In other words, the teacher maintains the academic flow without getting sidetracked by either student or teacher irrelevancies. Irrelevancies lead to what the Professional Orientation Program (POP) calls movement slowdown. A teacher irrelevancy is for example, if in the middle of a grammar lesson, the teacher remembers he or she is to get a count of students attending Friday's pep rally and says, "By the way, how many are going to the pep rally on Friday?" This type of discourse breaks the academic focus and leaves the student wondering what he or she should be thinking about—the grammar lesson or the pep rally. Additionally, this type of discourse alerts the students that academic focus is broken and the tendency for deviant behavior is increased. Effective teachers avoid this occurrence through well organized lessons with detailed plans. A more likely occurrence in today's classrooms is student irrelevancies. The POP advises teachers to utilize planned ignoring in this case. This teaches the class to ignore students who speak out and will usually result in the behavior fading over time.

Additionally, teachers should avoid scrambled discourse. The PMS Domains defines scrambled discourse as "discontinuous or garbled verbal behavior in which ideas are loosely associated." This happens when a teacher does not have a command of their subject matter. Effective teachers avoid this through detailed organized planning.

Another concept related to scrambled discourse and equally ineffective is the use of vagueness words. The PMS Domains defines vagueness words as "words of everyday speech which teachers often use to describe, to present information, or to answer questions and for which the denotations are indeterminate (e.g., something, a little, some, much, few, things, you see, perhaps, actually)." Hiller, Fisher, and Kaess, in a 1969 study, discovered a correlation between the use of vagueness words and the ineffectiveness of the lesson. Later research confirmed this relationship between the use of vagueness words and student achievement. Some examples of vagueness words are: somewhere, other people, not all, not many, as you all know, a bunch, aspects, factors, sorts, may, might, could be, probably, sometimes, and frequently. Teachers who avoid such words and phrases in their lectures are more effective which results in higher subject matter retention among the students.

Furthermore, the POP advises teachers that today's classrooms need high teacher direction to maintain academic focus. It suggests this is promoted through effective rule setting and monitoring. This leads to decreased deviant behavior which results in more academic focus.

Additionally, the POP suggests the discourse is controlled by planning for the relevance of the students. It advises the teacher to assume that all students are concrete learners. By doing this, the teacher is assured the cognitive base is in place before moving to higher level thinking processes necessary for the lesson to be understood.

Furthermore, teachers should never pose complex questions. Doing this causes the student to lose his or her train of thought resulting in off-task behavior. It is more effective to pose a single question, pause for student comprehension, and then choose a respondent to answer. This results in a clear progression of the lesson that the students can more easily comprehend.

Therefore, effective teachers focus teacher and student talk on the subject matter through connected discourse, clear directions, teaching to the concrete learner, and only posing single questions. Effective teachers also avoid vagueness words and teacher irrelevancies while dealing with student irrelevancies effectively.

SKILL 14.3 Manages transitions from one activity to another in a systematic, academically oriented way.

Effective teachers use class time efficiently. This results in higher student subject engagement and will likely result in more subject matter retention. One way teachers use class time efficiently is through a smooth transition from one activity to another. The Florida Performance Measurement System: Domains (FPMS Domains) labels this activity as "management transition." Management transition is defined as "teacher shifts from one activity to another in a systemic, academically oriented way." One factor that contributes to efficient management transition is the teacher's management of instructional material. FPMS Domains defines management of instructional material as "teacher preparation of materials that are to be used for a particular segment of instruction readily available." Effective teachers gather their materials during the planning stage of instruction. Doing this, a teacher avoids flipping through things looking for the items necessary for the current lesson. Momentum is lost and student concentration is broken when this occurs. This is also the ideal time for deviant behaviors to occur.

Additionally, teachers who keep students informed of the sequencing of instructional activities maintains systematic transitions because the students are prepared to move on to the next activity. The FPMS Domains defines sequencing of instructional activity as "teacher cites an order or pattern for a series of activities." For example, the teacher says, "When we finish with this guided practice together, we will turn to page twenty-three and each student will do the exercises. I will then circulate throughout the classroom helping on an individual basis. Okay, let's begin." Following an example such as this will lead to systematic smooth transitions between activities because the students will be turning to page twenty-three when the class finishes the practice without a break in concentration.

Another method that leads to smooth transitions is to move students in groups and clusters rather than one by one. The Florida Professional Orientation Program calls this "group fragmentation." For example, if some students do seat work while other students gather for a reading group, the teacher moves the students in pre-determined groups. Instead of calling the individual names of the reading group, which would be time consuming and laborious, the teacher simply says, "Will the blue reading group please assemble at the reading station. The red and yellow groups will quietly do the vocabulary assignment I am now passing out." As a result of this activity, the classroom is ready to move on in a matter of seconds rather than minutes.

Additionally, the teacher may employ academic transition signals. The FPMS Domains defines academic transition signals as a "teacher utterance that indicate[s] movement of the lesson from one topic or activity to another by indicating where the lesson is and where it is going." For example, the teacher may say, "That completes our description of clouds, now we will examine weather fronts." Like the sequencing of instructional materials, this keeps the student informed on what is coming next so they will move to the next activity with little or no break in concentration.

Therefore, effective teachers manage transitions from one activity to another in a systemically oriented way through efficient management of instructional matter, sequencing of instructional activities, moving students in groups and by employing academic transition signals. Through an efficient use of class time, achievement is increased because students spend more class time engaged in on-task behavior.

SKILL 14.4 Establishes procedures to be followed by students who are tardy, who must leave and return to class, who are without materials, etc.

Effective teachers have rules that deal with controlled interruptions. The Performance Measurement System: Domains (PMS Domains) defines controlled interruptions as a "teacher enforces rules and procedures to be followed by students who are tardy to class or who do not have their supplies, etc." The most efficient classrooms are run by teachers who give a high degree of directions. There is no better way to set the tone for this classroom atmosphere than by rule explication and monitoring. The PMS Domains defines rule explication and monitoring as a "teacher specifies rules of conduct, explains them, provides practice in their use, and consistently checks student conduct by the rules." For example, when a student returns to class after being absent, he or she places his or her parent note in the box on the teacher's desk designated for this. The student is aware that the teacher will deal with it after the class is engaged and when time allows. The student then proceeds to the side counter where extra copies of yesterday's work is located. The student takes the work and sits down to begin today's classwork. The student is aware that the teacher will deal with individual instructions during seat work time when it will not disrupt the class momentum. This is an example of rule explication because the teacher explained the procedures for this instance at the beginning of the year, and through constant monitoring the student is aware of what is expected of him or her in this situation. As a result of specifying classroom procedures for controlled interruptions, the classroom momentum is maintained and thus on-task time is increased. This will result in increased achievement because on-task time directly correlates to student achievement.

Therefore, effective teachers have rules in place dealing with controlled interruptions. The teacher has insured these rules will be followed through the use of rule explication and monitoring. The Professional Orientation Program advises beginning teachers that for a rule to be effective, the teacher must state the rule, explain the rule, lead the students through a guided practice of the rule and then consistently monitor the rule to insure compliance. The monitoring process is what teaches the student that they must also be consistent in these matters.

SKILL 14.5. Plans activities for students who complete classwork early.

The effective teacher is always prepared for all levels of student ability. The Professional Orientation Program instructs beginning teachers to gear student work to the mid line achievement level of the students, allowing extra time for the slower achieving students, and providing an enrichment handout for the higher achieving students who are done early. Effective teachers do this because it is not desirable to have students waiting for the next activity because off-task time leads to deviant behaviors. Additionally, in 1976, B. Bloom reviewed a number of student participation studies and found a positive correlation between student engagement and student achievement. Therefore, the effective teacher keeps all students on-task as much as possible.

The Performance Measurement System: Domains refers to keeping all students engaged as wait time avoidance. It defines wait time avoidance as "the teacher organizes the class to keep the lesson moving and provides structure for those students who finish classwork early, thereby eliminating the necessity for students to wait for teacher approval." For example, the teacher gives the directions for the science seat work, then the teacher says, "If you are done early, and are sure your answers are accurate, you should turn-in your paper and pick-up the additional worksheet on my desk." Another example would be for the teacher to say, "Those students who are done early are to check the accuracy of their answers and then turn-in their paper. Then, they are to review the vocabulary list for the test we will be taking tomorrow." Both of these instructions will keep the students who complete the seat work before the majority of the class engaged in classwork.

In conclusion, effective teachers keep all students engaged in classwork when the class is waiting for the slower students to finish the seat work. This is called wait time avoidance and is essential to the successful classroom because research shows that the longer a student is engaged in on-task behaviors, the more subject matter is retained.

SKILL 14.6 Established routines and procedures for such activities as passing out papers, moving to get books, and writing on the board, and has procedures worked out and materials prepared and in order.

Effective teachers deal with daily classroom procedures efficiently and quickly because then students will spend the majority of class time engaged in academic tasks which will likely result in higher achievement. Various studies have shown that the high achieving classrooms spend less time on off-task behavior. For example, C.W. Fisher, et al, in a 1978 study, found that in the average classroom, students spent about eight minutes an hour engaged in off-task behavior. However, this was reduced to about four minutes in high achieving classrooms. Therefore, effective teachers spend less time on daily housekeeping chores.

The Performance Measurement System: Domains (PMS Domains) defines housekeeping as "teacher routinizes activities such as passing papers out, moving to get books, writing on the board, etc., and has materials prepared, procedures worked out, and everything in order." It further advises that teachers presort papers into rows and have the first person in the row distribute them. This achieves the laborious task of passing back papers in a few minutes. This same technique is useful for distributing books. The teacher may ask the students in the first seat to pick up enough books for their row and pass them out. Using this technique keeps the majority of the students in their seats and achieves the task quickly. Another possibility would be for the teacher to place the proper number of books on the front desks while finishing the last lesson. In this case, students have been pre-instructed not to pass the books back until instructed to do so. Regardless of the technique employed by the teacher, it is important that it is pre-planned to utilize as little of class time as possible. Instructing the students of the daily routine activities early in the year leads to a more efficient use of class time on a daily basis.

Additionally, effective teachers have highly planned lessons with all materials in order prior to class. The PMS Domains refers to this as management of instructional material and defines it as "teacher preparation of materials that are to be used for a particular segment of instruction readily available." In other words, if a teacher is going to utilize a chart or a map in a lesson, the chart or map is already prepared and in place in the classroom before class begins. Furthermore, all materials are copied and in order ready to pass out as needed. This results in the efficient distribution of materials and leads to less off-task time.

Therefore, effective teachers routinize daily housekeeping activities to minimize the amount of time spent on them. Additionally, they have all materials prepared prior to class and in order to facilitate speedy distribution.

COMPETENCY 15.0 Communicates effectively using verbal and non-verbal skills

SKILL 15.1   Organizes sequences and presents ideas/materials using the basic principles of English at a level appropriate to students.

Effective teachers are well versed in the areas of cognitive development which is crucial to presenting ideas and or materials to students at a level appropriate to their developmental maturity. Effective teachers have the ability to use non-verbal and verbal patterns of communications which focus on age-appropriate instructions and materials.

Consistent with Piagean theory of Cognitive development, younger children (below age 8) have poor language competencies which result in a poor ability to solve complicated problems. Educational instructions and information should be saturated with simplified language to compensate for the limited language competencies of younger children. In contrast, older children (age 8 and older) have developed a greater ability to understand language and therefore are capable of solving complex problems. Older children are capable of understanding more advanced instructions and materials which require more advanced language skills.

As the classroom environment increasingly becomes a milieu saturated with cognitive, social, and emotional developmental levels and cultural diversity; the effective teacher must rise to the challenge of presenting ideas and materials appropriate for varying levels of students. Additionally, materials and ideas must be organized, sequenced, and presented to students in a manner consistent with the basic principles of English in a manner relevant to students as a whole.

SKILL 15.2   Listens effectively to messages, identifies relevant/irrelevant information, draws inferences, and summarizes the message(s).

The effective teacher uses advanced communication skills such as clarification, reflection, perception, and summarization as a means to facilitate communication. Teachers who are effective communicators are also good listeners. Teacher behaviors such as eye contact, focusing on student body language, clarifying students' statements, and using "I" messages are effective listeners.

The ability to communicate with students, listen effectively, identify relevant and non-relevant information, and summarize students' messages facilitates establishing and maintaining an optimum classroom learning environment.

SKILL 15.3. In oral presentation, modulates voice quality and level to add interest and stresses important information.

The Performance measurement System: Domains defines teacher's speech as the voice characteristic that make up the auditory stimuli as distinguished from the content or message of discourse. Speech patterns which are varied in intensity, rate of speech, and volume adds interests to teachers' oral presentations. Teacher discourse can have a positive effective on student achievement when the rate of speech is varied in intensity and volume with a moderate rate of speech (about 200 words/min.).

SKILL 15.4 In written presentation, (e.g., board work, letters to parents, etc.) applies basic mechanics of writing, spelling, capitalization, and punctuation.

The effective teacher serves as a role model for students, fellow teachers, and parents. Therefore, proper mechanics of writing, spelling, capitalization, and punctuation must be observed at all times. Teachers should use their experiences of presenting board work and writing letters to parents as opportunities to model the mechanics of writing, spelling, capitalization, and punctuation.

When teachers fail to correctly follow the basic mechanics of writing, spelling, capitalization, and punctuation, they communicate to students that good writing skills are not important. Proper planning of board work, and careful proof- reading of correspondences written to parents can facilitate the proper application of teacher writing presentations.

SKILL 15.5 Uses non-verbal communication to enhance student action and student performance.

The Performance Measurement System: Domains defines body language as teachers' facial or other body behavior that express interest, excitement, joy, and positive personal relations, or boredom, sadness, dissatisfaction, or negative personal relations, or else, no clear message at all.

The effective teacher communicates non-verbally with students by using positive body language, expressing warmth, concern, acceptance, and enthusiasm. Effective teachers augment their instructional presentations by using positive non-verbal communication such as smiles, open body posture, movement, and eye contact with students. The energy and enthusiasm of the effective teacher can be amplified through positive body language.

COMPETENCY 16.0 Creates and maintains academic focus by using verbal, nonverbal and for visual or motivational devices.

SKILL 16.1   Relates instructional objectives and activities to interests, feelings, capabilities, and experiences of students.

The major teaching functions include getting the class under way, providing instruction about what to do, developing the lesson, managing seat work, homework, practice, and conducting reviews. All of the functions require teachers to comprehend the aptitude and achievement of students, the appropriateness of subject matter, and the kinds of difficulties students may encounter as they try to learn.

Students' attitudes and perceptions about learning are the most powerful factors influencing academic focus and success. When instructional objectives center around students' interests and are relevant to their lives, effective learning occurs. Learners must believe that the tasks that they are asked to perform have some value and that they have the ability and resources to perform them. If a student thinks a task is unimportant, he will not put much effort into it. If a student thinks he lacks the ability or resources to successfully complete a task, even attempting the task becomes too great a risk. Not only must the teacher understand the students' abilities and interests, she must also help students develop positive attitudes and perceptions about tasks and learning.

Students generally do not realize their own abilities and frequently lack self-confidence. Teachers can instill positive self-concepts in children and thereby enhance their innate abilities by providing certain types of feedback. Such feedback includes attributing students' successes to their effort and specifying what the student did that produced the success. Qualitative comments influence attitudes more than quantitative feedback such as grades.

Despite a teacher's best efforts to provide important and appropriate instruction there may be times when a teacher is required to teach a concept, skill, or topic that students may perceive as trivial and irrelevant.. These tasks can be effectively presented if the teacher exhibits a sense of enthusiasm and excitement about the content. Teachers can help spark the students' interest by providing anecdotes and interesting digressions. Research indicates that as teachers become significantly more enthusiastic, students exhibit increased on-task behavior.

Teachers must avoid teaching tasks that fit their own interests and goals and design activities that address the students' concerns. In order to do this, it is necessary to find out about students and to have a sense of their interests and goals. Teachers can do this by conducting student surveys and simply by questioning and listening to students. Once this information is obtained the teacher can link students' interests with classroom tasks.

Teachers are learning the value of giving assignments that meet the individual abilities and needs of students. After instruction, discussion, questioning, and practice have been provided, rather than assigning one task to all students teachers are asking students to generate tasks that will show their knowledge of the information presented. Students are given choices and thereby have the opportunity to demonstrate more effectively the skills, concepts, or topics that they as individuals have learned. It has been established that student choice increases student originality, intrinsic motivation, and higher mental processes.

SKILL 16.2 Informs students about objectives, subsequent learning tasks, and performance expectations.

It is usually recognized that students must know what they are to do if learning activities are to be effective. Some teachers are unsure as to what to do or say in order to make sure that students understand what they are to do and how to do it. Obviously it is essential for teachers to help students understand and be clear about tasks. The clearer the students' understanding of objectives, the more effective instruction will be. Teachers must identify and articulate the specific behaviors that are expected during and after the completion of tasks. Research indicates that teachers who use techniques that ensure that assignments are understood and who hold students responsible for assignments are more likely to be successful than teachers who do not do these things.

If the teacher begins a lesson by providing orientation and direction and supports the lesson momentum by providing distinct explanations, checking for student comprehension of explanations, sustaining academic focus by transitions from one part of the lesson to another and providing practice where it is appropriate, then learning will be increased.

Explaining to students in advance the general framework of the lesson, or giving them some of the main ideas on which to relate subsequent learning, is said to facilitate learning. In other words, stating objectives at the beginning of the lesson and outlining the lesson content constitute an overview that eases study and achievement.

It is a matter of professional opinion that students are likely to achieve more when they know what they are expected to learn. Besides telling the students what they are going to learn, teachers may choose to use advance organizers which include visual motivations such as outlines, graphs, and models. This practice is especially valuable to the visual learner and is a motivational factor for most students.

Specific questions asked at the beginning of a lesson can also help students focus on the content and be more attentive to instruction. Once the lesson is underway it is further developed by additional questions as well as explanations, checking understanding, making transitions from one topic to another, and sometimes engaging in practice. Teachers who clearly explain difficult points during a lesson and then analyze problems utilizing questioning techniques with the students are more effective than those who do not.

SKILL 16.3   Modifies instructional strategies during learning activities based on students' responses and needs.

The value of teacher observations cannot be underestimated. It is through the use of teacher observations that the teacher is able to informally assess the needs of the students during instruction. These observations will drive the lesson and determine the direction that the lesson will take based on student activity and behavior. Teacher observations also set the pace of instruction and ascertain the flow of both student and teacher discourse. After a lesson is carefully planned, teacher observation is the single most important component of an instructional presentation.

One of the primary behaviors that teachers look for in an observation is on-task behavior. There is no doubt that student time on-task directly influences student involvement in instruction and enhances student learning. If the teacher observes that a particular student is not on-task, she will change the method of instruction accordingly. She may change from a teacher-directed approach to a more interactive approach. Questioning will increase in order to cull the participation of the students. If appropriate, the teacher will introduce manipulative materials to the lesson. In addition, teachers may switch to a cooperative group activity thereby removing the responsibility of instruction from the teacher and putting it on the students.

Teachers will also change instructional strategies based on the questions and verbal comments of the students. If the students express confusion or doubt or are unclear in any way about the content of the lesson, the teacher will immediately take another approach in presenting the lesson. Sometimes this can be accomplished by simply rephrasing an explanation. At other times, it will be necessary for the teacher to use visual organizers or models for understanding to be clear. Effective teachers are sensitive to the reactions and responses of their students and will almost intuitively know when instruction is valid and when it is not. Teachers will constantly check for student comprehension, attention, and focus throughout the presentation of a lesson.

After the teacher has presented a skill or concept lesson she will allow time for the students to practice the skill or concept. At this point it is essential for the teacher to circulate among the students to check for understanding. If the teacher observes that any of the students did not clearly understand the skill or concept, then she must immediately readdress the issue using another technique or approach.

SKILL 16.4 Uses reinforcement techniques to maintain on-task behavior and promote student motivation.

Many factors contribute to student on-task behavior including student interest in the content, student ability, student attitude and student needs. Teacher behavior can impact student behavior just as strongly as any other factor. It is imperative that teachers use strategies that encourage and maintain on-task behavior and be aware that they alone may be responsible for motivating students.

A natural way to reinforce on-task behavior is for the teacher to plan activities that reflect children's interests and build lessons based on children's ideas. Teachers guide students through lessons by responding to their questions and ideas, engaging them in conversation, and challenging their thinking.

Once a child-centered foundation has been established for presenting a lesson, the teacher must concentrate on maintaining student focus. To some degree teachers can rely on students' internal motivation to acquire competence. This internal motivation can be greatly affected by the teacher's attitude and enthusiasm. The teacher is a vital role model for promoting student motivation.

Questioning can help maintain focus, direct academic discussions, and create interactive instruction. Questioning can also reinforce content and sustain both on-task behavior and student motivation. Asking questions is a significant part of the instructional process and is most effective when it includes both simple comprehension questions and complex higher order thinking questions.

Teacher academic feedback exists in many forms including verbal response which can be an effective positive reinforcement and may contribute to students' on-task behavior. If academic feedback is specific, evaluative, and/or provides corrective information, then on-task behavior, student motivation, and achievement will increase. The most frequently used types of academic feedback are repeating what the student has said in an approving manner, calling on a student to further develop a response, and giving simple praise. Academic praise or specific statements that give information about the value of a student's response further add to student motivation and on-task behavior.

Academic feedback is also effective when written especially when it consists of specific comments on errors and is tempered by suggestions as to how the student may improve. It is most productive when it includes at least one positive remark on work well done. It is sometimes difficult to provide written feedback immediately and this delay reduces the effectiveness of the feedback. This is one area where a computer can be more dynamic than a teacher because the computer can provide immediate written feedback.

SKILL 16.5 Uses media to secure interest and maintain academic focus.

The use of media in lesson presentation has become an instructional staple. In order to address the many learning styles that are present within a classroom, the teacher must incorporate the use of media. In today's society where children have been stimulated and entertained by television, teachers must rely on this and other media to secure the interest of students.

A wide variety of media is available in most schools including overhead projectors, tape recorders, and videos. Other low technology media are important motivators in helping students maintain academic focus such as posters, graphs, matrices and charts. Not only are these visuals valuable as motivators, they are also organizers and assist the students in understanding and retaining information.

The implementation of media into instruction offers both the students and the teacher variety. There is "something for everybody". Teachers can be on the cutting edge and address all learning styles and all learners will be stimulated by something within the structure and presentation of the lesson.

Many sophisticated high technology media are now available and are being actuated on lesson presentations throughout our schools. Computers connected to televisions or LCD panels allow teachers to present information in all content areas including technology. Laser disc players connected to either computer monitors or televisions allow students to view a voluminous amount of visual material. Media is an integral tool in delivering instruction and is applied by both teachers and students. Media can never replace teachers but it can offer teachers alternative teaching strategies that students will respond to in a positive and enlightened manner.

SKILL 16.6 Uses students' ideas, talents and products to secure interest and maintain attention.

As previously stated, student learning increases when their interests and ideas are the focus of instruction. Undoubtedly, students learn more when they decide what they will learn because the desire to learn is already present. Not only should students be encouraged to decide what they will learn, they should also be given the opportunity to decide what methods they will use to learn. Frequently students have ideas as to how to acquire information and knowledge and how to demonstrate their understanding of newly acquired knowledge. More and more students are generating the tasks which will aid them in learning and in assessing what they have learned. Teachers are also capitalizing upon the talents of students to enhance instruction. Research indicates that many times students learn best from other students. It is natural for teachers to tap this valuable resource and to encourage students to share their expertise. Teachers are no longer the only nor even the most effective deliverer of information. Students can help one another by working together in cooperative groups or by engaging in peer tutoring activities as well as by giving presentations to the entire group.

Some of the most influential motivating resources that can stimulate learning are student products. The process of creating a product can be exhilarating to the student engaged in the learning activity. The actual creation of the finished product can be a strong motivator to other students due to the excitement of the student who created the product. Enthusiasm and excitement are contagious. Nothing is more rewarding to a teacher than to observe students who are excited about learning and who become absorbed in the process.

SKILL 16.7 Directs students' attention by use of verbal and nonverbal signals and cues.

Teachers' use of verbal and nonverbal cues is fundamental to instruction and student learning. These techniques are the simplest and most natural means of gaining student attention and are usually the first to be utilized. Verbal and nonverbal cues occur almost without the teacher's awareness. One of the most primary nonverbal motivators is eye contact. During the course of instruction, eye contact is sometimes the only cue necessary to regain a student's attention and re-establish academic focus. Another nonverbal cue that teachers use effectively is physical proximity. When the teacher notices that a student is not attentive, she will move closer to the student thereby regaining the student's attention. Teachers will also use gestures to motivate student interest and sustain student attention.

Verbal cues are integrated throughout each lesson and are usually used as a motivator to initiate interest at the beginning of a lesson. During the presentation of a lesson, the teacher will apply verbal cues which may include simply elevating or lowering her voice, calling students' names, or giving a group alert such as, "Listen to this." These cues are so automatic that they are perceived by the students to be a planned part of the instruction.

COMPETENCY 17.0 Presents forms of knowledge such as concepts, laws and law-like principles, academic rules, and value knowledge.

SKILL 17.1 Teaches concepts by providing or inducing definitions, examples, non-examples, and attributes, and by distinguishing related concepts.

Generally speaking, concepts can be taught in two manners: deductively or inductively. In a deductive manner, the teacher gives a definition along with one or two examples and one or two non-examples. As a means of checking understanding, the teacher will ask the students to give additional examples or non-examples and perhaps to repeat the definition. In an inductive manner, the students will derive the definition from examples and non-examples provided by the teacher. The students will test these examples and non-examples to ascertain if they possess the attributes that meet the criteria of the definition.

It cannot be assumed that students are gaining meaning through definitions. It is quite possible that some students are able to memorize definitions without actually understanding the concept. If students are understanding concepts and gaining meaning from definitions they will be able to apply this information by giving both examples and non-examples. Students will further be able to list attributes and recognize related concepts. Research indicates that when students gain knowledge through instruction which includes a combination of giving definitions, examples, non-examples, and by identifying attributes they are more likely to grasp complicated concepts than by other instructional methods.

Several studies have been carried out to determine the effectiveness of giving examples as well as the difference in effectiveness of various types of examples. It was found conclusively that the most effective method of concept presentation included giving a definition along with examples and non-examples and also providing an explanation of the examples and non-examples. These same studies indicate that boring examples were just as effective as interesting examples in promoting learning.

Additional studies have been conducted to determine the most effective number of examples which will result in maximum student learning. These studies concluded that a few thoughtfully selected examples are just as effective as several examples. It was determined that the actual number of examples necessary to promote student learning was relative to the learning characteristics of the learners. It was again ascertained that learning is facilitated when examples are provided along with the definition.

Learning is further enhanced when critical attributes are listed along with a definition, examples, and non-examples. Classifying attributes is an effective strategy for

FLORIDA TEACHER CERTIFICATION EXAM

both very young students and older students. According to Piaget's pre-operational phase of development, children learn concepts informally through experiences with objects just as they naturally acquire language. One of the most effective learning experiences with objects is learning to classify objects by a single obvious feature or attribute. Children classify objects typically, often without any prompting or directions. This natural inclination to classify objects carries over to classifying attributes of a particular concept and contributes to the student's understanding of concepts.

SKILL 17.2 Teaches laws or law-like principles by analyzing cause and effect, stating the causal principle or law, using linking words to connect effect(s) to cause(s), and by providing for application of law or principle.

In presenting explanatory knowledge, the teacher relates an outcome as is expected from a principle or law. This is a much more complicated teaching strategy and learning process than acquiring concepts. Students will not necessarily attain knowledge when the teacher states an academic law. It is essential for the teacher to explain the law in common terms that the students can easily understand. Often this explanation will be followed by a group discussion. Teachers can facilitate students' comprehension of laws or principles by analyzing causal conditions and their effects.

When teachers are explaining academic laws it is important to use linking words such as consequently, therefore, thus, in order to, etc. Research has been conducted which attests to the positive correlation between student academic achievement and the use of linking words by teachers. Using linking words clarifies the teacher's explanation and enhances the students' discussion. Linking words help the students see the relationship between the cause and effect and exemplify the "why" and "because".

Although students may be able to repeat an academic law or principle, the test for comprehension lies in the student's ability to apply the law to a specific situation or problem. Again, it is important to note that this process is much more difficult than comprehending a concept and should not be expected to be exhibited by very young students. Very young students - those still in Paige's pre-operational phase of development or those between four and seven years of age - are not able to think in terms of causal relationships in a methodical sense. Therefore, teachers of very young students will not give academic laws and need not be concerned with using linking words. Even when students know and understand an academic law, they frequently will not choose to apply it when solving a problem. Rather, students will primarily apply a law to that isolated situation for which the law was memorized.

SKILL 17.3 States academic rules, describes/analyzes the situation in which the rule applies, and provides for practice in applying the rule.

Teaching academic rules is a multi-step process. First the teacher may simply state the rule and follow up with an explanation and/or discussion as to the meaning of the rule. Next the teacher will provide examples of specific conditions to which the rule applies. Finally the teacher will provide exercises in applying the rule to similar conditions allowing the students the opportunity to practice academic rule application.

Academic rule application is similar to applying laws or law-like principles in that it is a higher level thinking exercise and involves both memory skills and abstract reasoning skills. It would be very difficult for the young student to first memorize an academic rule and then apply that rule to a variety of situations or conditions. In order to utilize academic rules effectively the teacher will use this strategy when instructing intermediate or older students. Only the simplest academic rules - such as those that apply to regrouping in mathematics - would be appropriate for young students.

Academic rules usually constitute part of course content such as grammar or mathematics. However, academic rules may also apply to sciences, be used as an instructional strategy for teaching the rules of behavior at the beginning of a school term.

SKILL 17.4 Teaches value knowledge by stating and exploring the value question, developing criteria of judgment, assembling facts, and testing the value judgment.

There are at least two types of value questions that the teacher must be concerned with: questions of practical value and questions of moral value. Practical value questions deal with objects, things, situations, etc. that can be put to good use. For example, scissors can be valued as either good or bad objects depending on how they are used. Moral value inheres to standards of rightness, goodness ethics, and virtues. For example, relating a conversation you have had with another person accurately is ethical but to purposely misrepresent a conversation by exaggerating is unethical. While practical and moral questions differ, they "depend upon similar procedures for their development and justification." (FPMS Domains, 1991)

Caution must be applied when considering moral questions which can be interpreted as value judgments. Teachers do not teach which values or morals are right, good, or even appropriate but rather facilitate students in becoming aware of their own values and in making changes in their own values as their thinking indicates. Including moral and value questions in class discussions will support students' positive self-concepts and may influence their constructive decisions and actions. Moral questions might be best sufficed if limited to discussions about appropriate classroom behavior and rules.

COMPETENCY 18.0   Presents directions appropriate for carrying out an instructional activity.

SKILL 18.1 Informs students of objectives, assessments and performance standards.

Teachers can use many tools to inform students of pertinent information such as unit objectives, planned assessments or minimum standards. Letters home, bulletin boards, verbal reminders, student copied notes and daily assignment journals are all useful for this purpose.

Objectives are most often stated at the start of a school term or semester. Many schools and counties have form letters or printed objectives that a teacher may choose to send home with a student. An introductory letter, customary at the start of a term, often will contain information on objectives.

Teachers may wish to start a unit with a list of objectives to be completed by the student during the unit. Remember also to inform students should class objectives be modified during the year.

As with objectives all formal assessments should be announced. To insure that a student is aware, teachers may wish to use more than one method. Verbal reminders plus a written reminder placed on a bulletin board or chalk board, will most likely be effective. Give students enough advanced warning so that they may plan study time at home or rearrange their schedules to prepare. School or county wide assessment, i.e. CTBS testing, is usually announced through school distributed letters.

Students should be made aware of the grading scale at the start of the school year. Before beginning an assignment, it is also useful to make the students aware of the standards you will be using to evaluate it and assign it a grade. Tests should include information on the point value of each question or section. Writing assignments should include a discussion on what must be included for the paper to be weighted high or low. The value of an assignment should also be discussed at the time it is assigned.

SKILL 18.2 Informs students of the sequence and nature of learning activities to achieve results the objectives.

Most assignments will require more than one educational principle. It is helpful to explain to students the proper order in which these principles must be applied to complete the assignment successfully. Subsequently students should also be informed of the nature of the assignment: cooperative learning, group project, individual assignment, etc. This is often done at the start of the assignment.

Direction should include important special instructions i.e. show all work, underline thesis statement. For more formal or complicated assignments, term papers, hands on art project, a step by step instructional guide developed by the teacher can be used along with a timetable to help the student stay on task.

SKILL 18.3 Informs students of the materials needed for a learning activity and explains their use.

Students cannot work effectively and teaching can be severely compromised should students be unprepared for a lesson. Any daily supplies should be discussed with students at the start of a school term. Any special supplies should be discussed far enough in advance to allow students time to obtain the needed items.

If materials will be required for completion of an assignment that are not usually used in the classroom, teachers should both inform students and parents of this verbally and in writing. Letters home, bulletin boards or written reminders in class in conjunction with frequent verbal reminders are helpful. When the teacher is ready to begin the assignment, students should be verbally reminded to get out the needed materials.

Any item that is new to a student or the class should be explained. For example, the first time students work with angles in geometry, the use of a protractor should be discussed, practiced and a comprehension check done. This eliminates a student's inability to use an item as a possible cause should they fail to successfully complete the assignment.

SKILL 18.4 Determines if students understand the directions.

Students are notorious for skipping the directions. Teachers can stress the importance of taking a moment to read and understand the directions but they should also check for comprehension themselves as part of the assignment process.

Verbal checks of the whole group can be done i.e. Does everyone understand what needs to be done? It is also advisable to individual checks i.e. John, where do you need to place your answers? or Anne, what must you do to get full credit for writing a complete thesis statement?

Teachers should also monitor the classroom at the start of an assignment to insure that all students are following the directions and are beginning to work on the assignment.

COMPETENCY 19. 0 Stimulates and directs student thinking, and checks student comprehension through appropriate questioning techniques.

SKILL 19.1 Orients students to classwork and provides transition statements.

Focusing students on the tasks to be completed will help both the teacher and the student. If a student understands exactly what is being done and what is coming up next he/she will be more likely to be on task and thinking at the same pace as the classroom.

A brief description, posted in a routine spot, is useful to orientate the class to the days objectives. A teacher may wish to discuss this with the class at the start of the day or period. Teachers may prefer to verbally inform students of the days activities i.e. Today we will be learning about the Boston Tea Party.

Since most days will consist of more than one task, teachers must clearly inform students of any transitions. This is easily done verbally through common transition statements i.e. Now we will work on the paper by ourselves. Next, get out your English text book and turn to page 30 so we can go over the exercises. We need to move on to silent reading time. If you have completed taking notes, get out your math book and begin the homework assignment.

SKILL 19.2 Asks low order and high order questions to effectively stimulate and direct a student's thinking.

Since most teachers want their educational objectives to use higher level thinking skills, teachers need to direct student to these higher levels on the taxonomy. Questioning is an effective tool to build up students to these higher levels.

Low order questions are useful to begin the process. They insure the student is focused on the required information and understands what need to be included in the thinking process. For example, if the objective is for students to be able to read and understand the story "Goldilocks and the Three Bears," the teacher may wish to start with low order questions, i.e. What are some things Goldilocks did while in the bears home? (knowledge) or Why didn't Goldilocks like the Papa Bears chair?

Through a series of questions, the teacher can move the students up the taxonomy. If Goldilocks had come to your house what are some things she may have used? (application) How might the story differed if Goldilocks had visited the three fishes? (synthesis) Do you think Goldilocks was good or bad? Why? (evaluation) The teacher through questioning can control the thinking process of the class. As students become more involved in the discussion they are systematically being lead to higher level thinking.

COMPETENCY 20.0   Provides appropriate practice to promote learning and retention.

SKILL 20.1   Varies the structure, duration, and nature of practice activities, based upon complexity of material and ability of the learner.

Student learning is an intricate, multi-faceted process. Teachers instruct based upon their students' background knowledge. The first step teachers may take in approaching a new topic or skill is to simply ask the students what they already know and list their responses. This will provide the teacher with a beginning point from which they can build instruction. The next step will include the teacher's delivery of the topic, subject matter, or skill information. These issues have been previously discussed at great length and in detail (see sections 1 through 19). Following these steps, the teacher will always provide time and resources for student practice. Student practice is perhaps the most crucial means by which information is internalized.

There are unlimited forms of practice. Just as the teacher intricately planned his/her instructional delivery based upon student needs, the teacher will also carefully plan the practice activities necessary to enhance the learning experience. These practice activities will depend largely on the students' developmental stage and on the skill or knowledge being practiced. Although practice activities are intended to reinforce what the teacher has taught, for many students the practice - the interactive process of doing something - is the point at which learning occurs. Therefore, the importance of practice activities cannot be underestimated. Teachers must monitor students as they practice in order to observe difficulties that might arise as well as student proficiency. Based on the observations teachers make during practice activities, it will be evident when additional instruction needs to occur and when the students are ready to go on to another concept or skill.

SKILL 20.2 Reinforces retention of specific information or skill by directing students to respond individually and/or together.

For some skill practice, such as basic addition, subtraction, and multiplication facts, the teacher will ask the students to respond orally either individually or chorally. This is a simple skill drill exercise and can be very effective in assisting children in memorizing facts. This process can also be effective in facilitating students in memorizing other law-like principles or academic rules.

Another important strategy in aiding student retention of information is questioning. Teacher questioning can be very effective in helping students retain a variety of information and is not limited to basic skills. Some of the reasons that teachers ask questions are: to arouse interest and to motivate students to participate actively, to review and summarize information that has been presented, and to help students see how concepts, knowledge, and skills can be applied. All of these reasons help students to internalize material.

SKILL 20.3 Provides a variety of activities for repetitive practice to promote learning and retention.

Repetitive practice can occur in many forms. Sometimes the teacher will lead the students in choral chants whereby they repeat basic skills including addition, subtraction, and multiplication facts. This activity can also be effective in memorizing spelling words and academic laws. In addition to orally repeating information, these same kinds of skills can be acquired by students by repeatedly writing multiplication tables, addition or subtraction facts, or spelling words. Older students may use these types of practice in memorizing algebraic formulas, geometric theorems, and scientific laws.

Repetitive practice may also occur over time. Teachers and students may revisit skills, concepts, or knowledge throughout a school year or even over several school years as a means of internalizing important information. Repetition may come in the form of discussing, rereading, or taking information to a higher level.

SKILL 20.4 Circulates and assists students during seat work to check comprehension and provide assistance.

The time that students spend doing seat work can be prime learning time. Some students actually learn more when they are left to explore and discover on their own. Sometimes learning is enhanced when students can work at their own pace and at their own speed. When students work independently the pressure to perform is removed and again learning increases. Most importantly, seat work time allows the teacher to circulate among the students making meaningful observations and providing the opportunity to give one-on-one instruction. For some students, this one-on-one instruction is vital to their learning. By circulating during practice time or seat work activities, the teacher is available to the students at whatever level they deem necessary. For some students that will mean leaving them to work independently. For others it will mean answering a simple question, and for others it will mean providing in-depth instruction.

Also of significant importance is the opportunity that circulation provides to check the students' levels of comprehension, understanding, and material internalization. From these observations, the teacher can determine what instructional activities will follow and can plan accordingly.

SKILL 20.5 Provides massed and distributed practice activities to promote long term retention.

Most teachers are aware that short term retention is the first phase of long term retention. During the time period that short term retention is being actualized, instruction and practice are ongoing. Once it appears that a skill or concept has become internalized, the teacher plans for future follow-up activities which will foster long term retention. Long term retention is not the result of haphazard instruction, but rather is the result of deliberate and planned instruction. Just as assessment is ongoing so is instruction and learning.

One of the best uses of practice time is to assign homework activities which will permit students to both reinforce learning as well as to revisit skills and concepts. This allows the teacher to use classroom time for instruction of new ideas while giving the students opportunities as well as motivation to practice important skills or concepts. Sometimes, while working on homework assignments with the assistance of a parent, students will develop a broader comprehension of a concept. Also during this valuable time, students may realize valid questions which can then be addressed during class time.

COMPETENCY 21.0 Relates to students' verbal communications in ways that encourage participation and maintains academic focus

SKILL 21.1 Shows acceptance and value of student responses by seeking clarification, elaboration, or uses students' comments to foster or redirect further discussion.

Various studies have shown that learning is increased when the teacher acknowledges and amplifies the student responses. Additionally, this can be even more effective if the teacher takes one student's response and directs it to another student for further comment. When this occurs, the students acquire greater subject matter knowledge. This is due to a number of factors. One is that the student feels that he or she is a valuable contributor to the lesson. Another is that all students are forced to pay attention because they never know when they will be called on. The Performance Measurement System (PMS) Domains, calls this group-alert. The teacher achieves group alert by stating the question, allowing for a pause time for the students to process the question and formulate an answer, and then calling on someone to answer. If the teacher calls on someone before stating the question, the rest of the students tune-out because they know they are not responsible for the answer. The FPMS Domains advises the teacher to also alert the non-performers to pay attention because they may be called on to elaborate on the answer. Non-performers are defined as all the students not chosen to answer.

The idea of directing the student comment to another student is a valuable tool for engaging the lower achieving student. If the teacher can illicit even part of an answer from a lower-achieving student and then move the spotlight off of that student onto another student, the lower achieving student will be more likely to engage in the class discussion the next time. This is because they were not put "on the spot" for very long and they successfully contributed to the class discussion.

Additionally, according to the PMS Domains, the teacher shows acceptance and gives value to student responses by acknowledging, amplifying, discussing or restating the comment or question. The Professional Orientation Program (POP) points out that if you allow a student response, even if it is blurted out, you must acknowledge the student response and tell the student the quality of the response. For example: The teacher asks, "Is chalk a noun?" During the pause time a student says, "Oh, so my bike is a noun." Without breaking the concentration of the class, the teacher looks to the student, nods and then places his or her index finger to the lips as a signal for the student not to speak out of turn and then calls on someone to respond to the original question. If the blurted out response is incorrect or needs further elaboration, the teacher may just hold up his or her index finger as an indication to the student that the class will address that in a minute when the class is finished with the current question.

A teacher acknowledges a student response by commenting on it. For example,

FLORIDA TEACHER CERTIFICATION EXAM

the teacher states the definition of a noun, and then asks for examples of nouns in the classroom. A student responds, "My pencil is a noun." The teacher answers, "Okay, let us list that on the board." By this response and the action of writing "pencil" on the board, the teacher has just incorporated the student's response into the lesson.

A teacher may also amplify the student response through another question directed to either the original student or to another student. For example, the teacher may say, "Okay", giving the student feedback on the quality of the answer, and then add, "What do you mean by "run" when you say the battery runs the radio?"

Another way of showing acceptance and value of student response is to discuss the student response. For example, after a student responds, the teacher would say, "Class, let us think along that line. What is some evidence that proves what Susie just stated."

And finally, the teacher may restate the response. For example, the teacher might say, "So you are saying, the seasons are caused by the tilt of the earth. Is this what you said?"

Therefore, a teacher keeps students involved by utilization of group-alert. Additionally, the teacher shows acceptance and value of student responses by acknowledging, amplifying, discussing or restating the response. This contributes to maintaining academic focus.

SKILL 21.2 Ignores or redirects digressions without devaluing student response.

The Professional Orientations Program explains that the focus of the classroom discussion should be on the subject matter and controlled by teacher-posed questions. When a student response is correct, it is not difficult to maintain academic focus. However, when the student response is incorrect, this task is a little more difficult. The teacher must redirect the discussion to the task at hand, and at the same time not devalue the student response. It is risky to respond in a classroom.

If a student is ridiculed or embarrassed by an incorrect response, the student my shut down and not participate thereafter in classroom discussion. One way to respond to the incorrect answer is to ask the child, "Show me from your book why you think that." This gives the student a chance to correct the answer and redeem himself or herself. Another possible response from the teacher is to use the answer as a non-example. For example, after discussing the characteristics of warm-blooded and cold-blooded animals, the teacher asks for some examples of warm-blooded animals. A student raises his or her hand and responds, "A snake." The teacher could then say, "Remember, snakes lay eggs; they do not have live birth. However, a snake is a good non-example of a mammal." The teacher then draws a line down the board and under a heading of "non-example" writes "snake". This action conveys to the child that even though the answer was wrong, it still contributed positively to the class discussion. Notice how the teacher did not digress from the task of listing warm-blooded animals, which in other words is maintaining academic focus, and at the same time allowed the student to maintain dignity.

It is more difficult for the teacher to avoid digression when a student poses a non-academic question. For example, during the classroom discussion of Romeo and Juliet, the teacher asks "Who told Romeo Juliet's identity?" A student raises his or her hand and asks, "May I go to the rest room?" The teacher could respond in one of two ways. If the teacher did not feel this was a genuine need, he or she could simply shake his or her head no while repeating the question, "Who told Romeo Juliet's identity?" If the teacher felt this was a genuine need and could not have waited until a more appropriate time, he or she may hold up the index finger indicating "just a minute", and illicit a response to the academic question from another student. Then during the next academic question's pause-time the teacher could hand the student the bathroom pass.

Using hand signals and body language to communicate with one student while still talking to the rest of the class demonstrates effective teacher withitness. According to The Palm Beach County Professional Orientation Program, this is the behavior that demonstrates to the students that the teacher knows what he or she is doing. More specifically, in this case it is overlapping-withitness. This is the ability to do two tasks at once. Moreover, it is maintaining academic focus with the class while attending to the needs of the one student who needs to use the rest room or go to the clinic. During the academic day, many non-academic tasks need to be attended to. If the students learn early on that the teacher is not side- tracked by these interruptions, they will stay on task and greater subject matter acquisition will occur.

The teacher may opt to ignore questions that are posed to throw the class off-task. For example, in response to an academic question the student asks, "What time does the bell ring?" The teacher may respond by shaking his or her head no and calling on someone else to answer the academic question. Under no circumstances should the student posing the non-academic question be given an answer. Otherwise, this is rewarding deviant behavior and will result in a loss of academic focus.

Therefore, a teacher can ignore or redirect digressions without devaluing student responses by allowing the student to correct the answer or by using the answer as a non-example. Furthermore, teacher can deal with non-academic interruptions through effective use of overlapping-withitness

COMPETENCY 22.0 Makes specific statements that indicate what was praiseworthy about, or the implications of, students' responses.

SKILL 22.1 and 22.2

The Professional Orientation Program points out that the reason for praise in the classroom is to increase the desirable in order to eliminate the undesirable. This refers to both conduct and academic focus. It further states that effective praise should be authentic, it should be used in a variety of ways, and it should be low-keyed. The Performance Measurement System (PMS) Domains, defines academic praise as specific statements that give information about the value of the response or its implications. For example, a teacher using academic praise would respond, "That is an excellent analysis of Twain's use of the river in Huckleberry Finn." Whereas a simple positive response to the same question would be: "That's correct."

SKILL 22.3 Corrects students' errors by giving a correction, or by providing an explanation of the error, providing information, or asking additional questions which would enable students to correct their own errors.

The Professional Orientation Program informs the beginning teacher that if academic feedback is specific, evaluates the student's answer, and gives the student corrective information, then achievement will increase. Effective teachers give immediate feedback and as a result clear up any misconceptions the students might have about the answer. Feedback may be the teacher explaining the problem with the answer, or it may be the teacher asking the student questions until the student reaches the correct answer.

The Performance Measurement System (PMS) Domains defines Correctives as the teacher providing an explanation of the error and giving a correction. For example, the teacher asks the class for a list of verbs. A student answers, "car". The teacher replies, "No, remember, we said a verb shows action. Do you remember what action is?" The student replies, "Yes, it's doing something." The teacher answers, "Yes, that is correct. Does a car show action?" The student answers, "No." The teacher replies, "No, it doesn't. But what action do we do with a car?" The student answers, "Drive." The teacher responds, "Yes, that is correct. Driving is the action we do with a car, therefore "drive" is a verb. Could you write "drive" on the board, please." In this example, the student was led to the correct answer through a series of questions. This technique allows the student to contribute positively to the class, even when he or she is unsure of the answer or has the wrong answer. This leads to more student participation which directly results in greater subject matter retention.

Redirects is another technique the Professional Orientation Program teaches new teachers. PMS Domains defines redirects as when the teacher asks a different student to answer the question or to react to the response. For example, a teacher asks, "What is the topic sentence in this paragraph?" A student replies, "Tom had a party." The teacher asks a second student, "Do you agree with that answer?" The second student replies, "Yes." The teacher then has two choices. He or She may either comment on the appropriateness of the answer, or ask the class if anyone disagrees with the first two students. This technique keeps the students actively involved in the analyzation process rather than having them tune out when they had been given the correct answer. This is because, at this point, the students are not sure if the first answer was correct or not. Therefore they must stay involved until the entire class has reached a consensus. This type of probing can lead to more student inferences. E. Abraham, M. Nelson and W. Reynolds explained, in a paper presented to the American Educational Research Association in New York in 1971, that they found this to be true. They examined this type of probing in grades one, six and eleven during social studies and math classes. They also discovered that the effects were increased in higher-achieving students. This could be partly due to the teacher. W. B. Dalton noted in a 1971 study that teachers, in a normal classroom setting, gave more than twice as many positive interactions to their higher-achieving students as they did to their lower-achieving students.

In summary, using correctives and redirects in the classroom leads to greater student involvement. This correlates to higher level thinking by the students and results in more subject matter retention. The effective teacher is aware of how and when these techniques are used in the classroom.

COMPETENCY 23.0 Reviewing material

SKILL 23.1 Engages students in an end-of-lesson recap, summary or review of subject matter. Engages students in weekly and monthly reviews to ensure long-term retention.

There are three types of reviews. The Performance Measurement System, (PMS) Domains refers to these as lesson-initiating reviews, topic summary within lesson reviews and lesson-end reviews. The effective teacher utilizes all three together with comprehension checks to make sure the students are processing the information. Rebecca Simmons found alternating between the lesson and ongoing assessment demonstrates the essence of learning.

The PMS Domains defines lesson-end reviews as a restatement (by the teacher or teacher and students) of the content of discussion at the end of a lesson.

For example, the teacher states "Class, we have just finished reading "Romeo and Juliet". Let us recap the specific breakdowns in communication that led to this tragic ending. Remember we commented on these as we read the literature." In this example, the teacher is checking for comprehension at the same time because the students are doing the summarizing for the lesson-end review.

In another example of lesson-end review, the teacher says, "Okay, students, please check your notes and make sure you have these incidents of breakdowns in communication that led to the tragedy of "Romeo and Juliet". The teacher lists the incidents either verbally or on the board.

Additionally, the research shows that effective teachers use reviews and recaps on a daily basis in the classroom. T. Good and D.A. Grouws determined the effectiveness of forty teachers by looking at the achievement records of their students from various classes. They established a list of key variables that separates the effective teachers from the ineffective teachers.   The list includes a daily review covering the concepts and skills contained in the homework, giving further practice while the teacher deals with the homework, followed by a comprehension check of the homework concepts before preceding with the day. Also on the list of key concepts are special reviews conducted weekly and monthly. The weekly reviews are conducted every Monday morning and focus on the skills and concepts of the previous week. The monthly reviews are conducted once a month and focus on skills and concepts from the previous month's lessons. Moreover, they reported the teachers utilizing the reviews to complement daily learning were significantly more successful in inducing student subject matter retention than the ineffective teachers.

The idea of regularly scheduled reviews is encouraged by The Palm Beach County Professional Orientation Program (PBC POP). The PBC POP advises beginning teachers to maintain a structured classroom. This is because too many of today's students come from disjointed families. It is possible that the only structure in a student's life may be in the classroom. Therefore, doing a daily review of the homework for the first few minutes of class followed by a few minutes of practice sets up a routine that the student can feel comfortable with. Moreover, when students know what is coming next, and what is expected of them, they feel more a part of their learning environment and deviant behavior is lessened.

Similarly, J.M. Kallison, Jr. found subject matter retention increased when lessons included an outline at the beginning of the lesson and a summary at the end of the lesson. This type of structure is utilized in successful classrooms.

Consequently, the teacher who has regularly scheduled reviews coupled with comprehension checks maintains a successful classroom.

COMPETENCY 24.0 Constructs items and tests according to recognized criteria.

SKILL 24.1 Identifies, selects, and constructs test items and tasks that appropriately assess mastery of an objective.

The purpose for testing the students is to determine the extent to which the instructional objectives have been met. Therefore, the test items must be constructed to achieve the desired outcome from the students. Gronlund and Linn advise that effective tests begin with a test plan that includes the instructional objectives and subject matter to be tested, as well as the emphasis each item should have. Having a test plan will result in valid interpretation of student achievement.

After determining the content of the test, a teacher selects appropriate test items. The test items used in typical classroom tests are either objective questions or essay questions. In an objective question, the student must either supply the answer or select the answer from a number of choices. In the supply answer type of objective question, the student typically writes a short answer. For example, "_____is the author of Moby Dick" or "who is the author of Moby Dick?" is a short answer question. The drawback to this test item is the possible ambiguity of student supplied answers.

Another common form of objective question is the true/false test item. Gronlund and Linn point out some limitations to this test item is its susceptibility to guessing, the difficulty involved in constructing a true/false item that is valid, and the limited specific learning outcomes it can measure. However, they also point out its usefulness in identifying cause and effect relationships as well as distinguishing fact and opinion.

A third form of test item is the matching exercise. An advantage of this type of test item is its ability to test large blocks of material in a short time. The major problem with this type of test item is its emphasis on memorization. Kenneth H. Hoover does not favor this type of test item, but points out that it can be appropriate when the exercise contains at least five, but not more than twelve items, uses only homogeneous items, and contains at least three extra answers to choose from.

The most commonly used objective question where the student chooses an answer is the multiple choice question. The multiple-choice test item consists of a stem and a list of responses, of which only one is the best answer. The responses which are not the answer are called distractors. Gronlund and Linn point out that multiple-choice test items are most useful for specific learning outcomes that utilize the students ability to understand or interpret factual information. Since the multiple-choice test item can be adopted to most subject matter, and because of its versatile nature, it is the most commonly used item on standardized tests. However, as Gronlund and Linn point out, the multiple-choice test item cannot test the ability to organize and present ideas.

The best way to test the student's ability to organize and present ideas is with the essay test item. This type of test item also utilizes the students ability to think and problem solve. However, the main drawbacks to this type of question are the unreliability of scoring and the amount of time necessary to score the item. Nevertheless, it is valuable when the specific learning outcomes cannot be measured any other way.

Therefore, it is true that all test items have useful purposes as well a drawbacks. It is important to keep the specific learning outcome and the subject matter covered in mind when constructing each item. The effective teacher evaluates and re-evaluates each test item with each test presentation.

SKILL 24.3 Identifies criteria for standards of performance.

The teacher determines the specific outcomes the students will be required to perform and writes them as specific learning outcome statements. An example of a specific learning outcome is "Identifies nouns in a sentence". The action the student will be required to perform is "identify". The teacher then sets the mastery level for this performance. For example, the teacher may say that the student will identify four out of five nouns in a sentence to achieve mastery. This, then sets the mastery level at eighty percent because four out of five correct is eighty percent. In other words, the teacher has set the standards of performance for this specific learning outcome at eighty percent.

Gronlund and Linn explained that for a teacher to know that the classroom test will measure the appropriate student performances based on the instructional learning outcomes, specifications should be used. They suggest the teacher build a "table of specifications". This may also be called a "test blueprint". A table of specifications is a two-way chart that shows the specific learning outcomes that a student must perform in order to pass the class. This is constructed by placing the instructional objectives along the top of the chart, and the subject matter content along the side of the chart, and placing the number of items devoted to each task in the boxes formed from the intersections of the objectives and the subject matter content. This is the same model used for valid test construction. As already established, students must perform the intended outcomes based on the standards the teacher set forth in the instructional objectives. In other words, if the mastery standard for a particular specific learning outcome is eighty percent, then the student must perform the task at the level of eighty percent to achieve mastery. For example, if the specific learning outcome is "defines the parts of speech", then the student must get eighty percent of the answers correct for the teacher to consider that the student has mastered the outcome. If the mastery level is eighty percent, then eighty percent correct on the test would be an "A". An effective teacher keeps the needs of each student in mind when setting standards of performance.

In conclusion, when the teacher "identifies criteria for standards of performance", he or she is predetermining the level of performance required of the students to receive a passing grade.

SKILL 24. 4 **Evaluates and revises tests on the basis of content validity, reliability, and student responses.**

Skill 1. **Demonstrate the ability to diagnose, assess, evaluate, and prescribe instruction in all subject areas, according to each child's readiness level.**

The concept of readiness is generally regarded as a developmentally-based phenomenon. Various abilities, whether cognitive, affective, or psychomotor, are perceived to be dependent upon the mastery or development of certain prerequisite skills or abilities. Readiness, then, implies that the necessary prior knowledge, experience, and developmental components are in place. A student lacking in one or more of the readiness prerequisites should not engage in the new task until first acquiring the necessary readiness foundation.

It should be noted, then, that a concept such as "readiness to learn" is too broad to be meaningful. Readiness needs to be considered in terms of readiness to "learn science" or, even more accurately, readiness to "learn photosynthesis". Since it is not feasible for the classroom teacher to assess each student's readiness for each lesson, mastery of one lesson is generally assumed to imply readiness for the next sequential lesson.

However, at each grade level, there exist readiness expectations and assumptions based on the previous year's instruction. Students who have not yet mastered those concepts are not ready to progress. Failure on the part of the teacher to address student deficiencies may lead to failure of the student to learn the new material.

Readiness for subject area learning is dependent not only on prior knowledge, but also on affective factors such as interest, motivation, and attitude. These factors are often more influential on student learning than the pre-existing cognitive base.

PURPOSES FOR ASSESSMENT

There are a number of different classification systems used to identify the various purposes for assessment. A compilation of several lists identifies some common purposes such as the following:

1) Diagnostic assessments are used to determine individual weaknesses and strengths in specific areas.

2) Readiness assessments measure prerequisite knowledge and skills.

FLORIDA TEACHER CERTIFICATION EXAM

3) <u>Interest and Attitude</u> assessments attempt to identify topics of high interest or areas in which students may need extra motivational activities.

4) <u>Evaluation</u> assessments are generally program or teacher focused.

5) <u>Placement</u> assessments are used for purposes of grouping students or determining appropriate beginning levels in leveled materials.

6) <u>Formative</u> assessments provide on-going feedback about student progress and the success of instructional methods and materials.

7) <u>Summative</u> assessments define student accomplishment with the intent to determine the degree of student mastery or learning that has taken place.

For most teachers, assessment purposes vary according to the situation. It may be helpful to consult several sources to help formulate an overall assessment plan. Kellough and Roberts (1991) identify six purposes for assessment. These are:

1) To evaluate and improve student learning.
2) To identify student strengths and weaknesses.
3) To assess the effectiveness of a particular instructional strategy.
4) To evaluate and improve program effectiveness.
5) To evaluate and improve teacher effectiveness.
6) To communicate to parents their children's progress. (p.341)

PRINCIPLES OF ASSESSMENT

Depending on the age of the student and the subject matter under consideration, diagnosis of readiness may be accomplished through pre-tests, checklists, teacher observation, or student self-reports. Diagnosis serves two related purposes--to identify those students who are not ready for the new instruction, and to identify for each student what prerequisite knowledge is lacking.

Student assessment is an integral part of the teaching-learning process. Identifying student, teacher, or program weaknesses is only significant if the information so obtained is used to remedy those concerns. Lesson materials and lesson delivery must be evaluated to determine relevant prerequisite skills and abilities. The teacher must be capable of determining whether a student's difficulties lie with the new information or with a lack of significant prior knowledge. The ultimate goal of any diagnostic or assessment endeavor is improved learning. Thus, instruction is adapted to the needs of the learner based on assessment information.

As is the case with purposes of assessment, there are a number of lists identifying principles of assessment. Linn and Gronlund (1995) identify five principles of assessment.

1) Clearly specifying what is to be assessed has priority in the assessment process.
2) An assessment procedure should be selected because of its relevance to the characteristics or performance to be measured.
3) Comprehensive assessment requires a variety of procedures.
4) Proper use of assessment procedures requires an awareness of their limitations.
5) Assessment is a means to an end, not an end in itself. (p. 6)

Stiggins (1997) introduces seven guiding principles for classroom assessment.

1) Assessments require clear thinking and effective communication.
2) Classroom assessment is key.
3) Students are assessment users.
4) Clear and appropriate targets are essential.
5) High-quality assessment is a must.
6) Understand personal implications.
7) Assessment as teaching and learning. (p. 11)

TYPES OF ASSESSMENT

It is also useful to consider the types of assessment procedures which are available to the classroom teacher. The types of assessment discussed below represent many of the more common types, but the list is not comprehensive.

Anecdotal records. These are notes recorded by the teacher concerning an area of interest or concern with a particular student. These records should focus on observable behaviors and should be descriptive in nature. They should not include assumptions or speculations regarding affective areas such as motivation or interest. These records are usually compiled over a period of several days to several weeks.

Rating scales & checklists. These assessments are generally self-appraisal instruments completed by the students or observation-based instruments completed by the teacher. The focus of these is frequently on behavior or affective areas such as interest and motivation.

Portfolio assessment. The use of student portfolios for some aspect of assessment has become quite common. The purpose, nature, and policies of portfolio assessment vary greatly from one setting to another. In general, though, a student's portfolio contains samples of work collected over an extended period of time. The nature of the subject, age of the student, and scope of the portfolio, all contribute to the specific mechanics of

FLORIDA TEACHER CERTIFICATION EXAM   121

analyzing, synthesizing, and otherwise evaluating the portfolio contents.

In most cases, the student and teacher make joint decisions as to which work samples go into the student's portfolio. A collection of work compiled over an extended time period allows teacher, student, and parents to view the student's progress from a unique perspective. Qualitative changes over time can be readily apparent from work samples. Such changes are difficult to establish with strictly quantitative records typical of the scores recorded in the teacher's grade book.

Questioning. One of the most frequently occurring forms of assessment in the classroom is oral questioning by the teacher. As the teacher questions the students, she collects a great deal of information about the degree of student learning and potential sources of confusion for the students. While questioning is often viewed as a component of instructional methodology, it is also a powerful assessment tool.

Tests. Tests and similar direct assessment methods represent the most easily identified types of assessment. Thorndike (1997) identifies three types of assessment instruments:
1) standardized achievement tests
2) assessment material packaged with curricular materials
3) teacher-made assessment instruments
    -pencil-and-paper tests
    -oral tests
    -product evaluations
    -performance tests
    -affective measures (p. 199).

Kellough and Roberts (1991) take a slightly different perspective. They describe "three avenues for assessing student achievement: (1) what the learner says;...(2) what the learner does;...and, (3) what the learner writes ..." (p. 343).

Types of tests. Formal tests are those tests which have been standardized on a large sample population. The process of standardization provides various comparative norms and scales for the assessment instrument. The term "informal tests" includes all other tests. Most publisher-provided tests and teacher-made tests are informal tests by this definition. Note clearly that an "informal" test is not necessarily unimportant. A teacher-made final exam, for example, is informal by definition because it has not been standardized.

STEPS IN THE ASSESSMENT PROCESS

There are several necessary steps to any effective assessment process in an instructional setting.

1) Determine what to assess.
2) Decide when to assess.
3) Determine how to assess.
4) Score or rate the assessment data.
5) Determine what conclusions and generalizations are appropriate.
6) Share the results with others as is appropriate.

In practice, these steps are not sequential, to be completed in a pre-determined order. They are interactive; each decision has bearing on the other steps. The goals and objectives of the lesson should directly determine what is to be assessed. The purpose of the assessment will indicate when one should assess. The methods used for instructional delivery should be reflected in the how to assess. Analyzing the results of an assessment requires consideration of validity and reliability of the assessment tool. Many abuses of assessment occur in the misapplication of results. A paper-and-pencil test, for example, can only assess knowledge of laboratory rules and procedures. It cannot assess the student's ability to actually follow or observe them. Finally, results should be shared only with those who have legitimate need or reason to know. The way in which the results are described or reported should be consistent with the background and knowledge of the listener to avoid potential misunderstandings.

VALIDITY & RELIABILITY

A desirable assessment is both reliable and valid. Without adequate reliability and validity, an assessment provides unusable results. A reliable assessment provides accurate and consistent results; there is little error from one time to the next. A valid assessment is one which tests what it intends to test.

Reliability is directly related to correlation. A perfect positive correlation equals +1.00 and a perfect negative correlation equals -1.00. The reliability of an assessment tool is generally expressed as a decimal to two places (eg. .85). This decimal number describes the correlation that would be expected between two scores if the same student took the test two times.

Actually, there are several ways to estimate the reliability of an instrument. The method which is conceptually the most clear is the test-retest method. When the same test is administered again to the same students, if the test is perfectly reliable, each student will receive the same score each time. Even as the scores of individual students vary some from one time to the next, it is desirable for the rank order of the students to

FLORIDA TEACHER CERTIFICATION EXAM

remain unchanged. Other methods of estimating reliability operate off of the same conceptual framework. Split-half methods divide a single test into two parts and compare them. Equivalent forms methods use two versions of the same test and compare them. With some types of assessments, such as essays and observation reports, reliability concerns also deal with the procedures and criteria used for scoring. This inter-rater reliability asks the question: how much will the results vary depending on who is scoring or rating the assessment data?

There are three commonly described types of validity: content validity, criterion validity, and construct validity. Content validity describes the degree to which a test actually tests, say, arithmetic. Story problems on an arithmetic test will lower its validity as a measure of arithmetic since reading ability will also be reflected in the results. However, note that it remains a valid test of the ability to solve story problems. Criterion validity is so named because of the concern with the test's ability to predict performance on another measure or test. For example, a college admissions test is highly valid if it predicts very accurately those students who will attain high GPAs at that college. The criterion in this case is college GPA. Construct validity is concerned with describing the usefulness or reality of what is being tested. The recent interest in multiple intelligence's, instead of a single IQ score, is an example of the older construct of intelligence being re-examined as potentially several distinct constructs.

Skill 2. Provide readiness activities in all subject areas, according to each child's readiness level.

A student's readiness for a specific subject is not an absolute concept, but is determined by the relationship between the subject matter or topic and the student's prior knowledge, interest, motivation, attitude, experience and other similar factors. Thus, the student's readiness to learn about the water cycle depends on whether the student already knows related concepts such as evaporation, condensation, and filtration. Readiness, then, implies that there is no "gap" between what the student knows and the prerequisite knowledge base for learning.

A pretest designed to assess significant and related prerequisite skills and abilities is the most common method of identifying the student's readiness. This assessment should focus, not on the content to be introduced, but on prior knowledge judged to be necessary for understanding the new content. A pretest which focuses on the new content may identify students who do not need the new instruction (who have already mastered the material), but it will not identify students with readiness gaps.

The most common areas of readiness concerns fall in the basic academic skill areas. Mastery of the basic skill areas is a prerequisite for almost all subject area learning. Arithmetic skills and some higher level mathematics skills are generally necessary for science learning or for understanding history and related time concepts. Reading skills are necessary throughout the school years and beyond. A student with poor reading skills is at a disadvantage when asked to read a textbook chapter independently. Writing skills, especially handwriting, spelling, punctuation, and mechanics, are directly related to success in any writing-based activity. A weakness in any of these basic skill areas may at first glance appear to be a difficulty in understanding the subject area. A teacher who attempts to help the student master the subject matter through additional emphasis on the content will be misusing instructional time and frustrating the student. An awareness of readiness issues helps the teacher to focus on treating the underlying deficiency instead of focusing on the overt symptoms.

Once a readiness gap has been identified, then the teacher can provide activities designed to close the gap. Specific activities may be of almost any form. Since most learning builds upon previous learning, there are few activities or segments of learning which can be viewed solely as readiness or non-readiness activities. In a very direct sense, all learning provides a level of readiness for additional learning. Simultaneously, very few types of learning can be identified as solely readiness activities without legitimacy in their own right.

Skill 3. Implement a program of curriculum and instruction that is developmentally appropriate.

While growth and maturation rates vary greatly from individual to individual, there are some generalizations which can be made concerning developmental characteristics of children. Most children appear to go through identifiable, sequential stages of growth and maturation, although not at the same rate. For the curriculum developers, it is often necessary to make some generalizations about the developmental level of the students of a particular age group or grade level. These generalizations, then, provide a framework for establishing the expectations of the children's performance. Textbooks, scope and sequence charts, school curriculum planners, and more, translate these generalizations into plans and expectations for the students. The curriculum plan that emerges identifies general goals and expectations for the "average" student.

One of the teacher's responsibilities in this situation is to realize the nature of the initial "rough estimate" of what is appropriate for a given group of students. The teacher should expect to modify and adjust the instructional program based on the needs and abilities of the students. A teacher may do this by grouping students for alternative instruction, adjusting or varying the materials (textbooks), varying the teaching methods, or varying the learning tasks.

CURRICULAR CONSIDERATIONS

The degree to which the classroom teacher has control over the curriculum varies from setting to setting. Some schools have precisely defined curriculum plans and teachers are required to implement the instruction accordingly. A more common occurrence is that the textbooks become the default curriculum. A fourth-grade arithmetic book, for example, defines what must be taught in fourth grade so that the fifth-grade teacher can continue the established sequence.

Whatever the source of limitations and requirements, the classroom teacher always has some control over the method of instruction and the use of supplemental materials and procedures. The teacher is responsible for implementing the formal curriculum and for providing necessary scaffolding to enhance student learning. Since the basic element of educational structure is time, the teacher must distribute the necessary learning activities over the available amount of time. The teacher can do this by creating an overview of what material is to be presented, the total amount of time available (whether for the school year, grading period, unit, etc.), the relative importance of the components of the material, and the students' prior knowledge of portions of the material.

LESSON PLANNING AND DELIVERY

Planning an individual lesson is a continuation of the principles for curriculum design. The same considerations exist, but on a smaller scale. Numerous lesson planning forms and guidelines are available. Some procedures are restricted to lessons of a particular nature, such as teaching a skill. Others are more generally applicable and provide a framework appropriate for most instruction. A typical lesson plan will include identification of objectives, the content, materials and supplies, instructional delivery methods, in-class reinforcement activities, homework assignments, evaluation of student learning, and evaluation of the lesson and teacher effectiveness.

There are three common methods by which a teacher may address grouping for instruction. Individualization requires extensive assessment both for placement and in an on-going capacity to monitor student progress and to plan subsequent instructional activities. Few teachers have the resources and time necessary to fully individualize their instructional program. A comprise approach is to assign students to small groups and then modify the lesson plans to reflect the needs of the group. This procedure offers some of the advantages of individualization without the extensive administrative demands. It is quite common, especially in content area instruction, for teachers to work with the whole class. This further reduces planning and management considerations and can help insure that all students are presented with the same information.

There are a number of procedures teachers can use to address the varying needs of the

FLORIDA TEACHER CERTIFICATION EXAM

students. Some of the more common procedures are:

1) <u>Vary assignments.</u> A variety of assignments on the same content allows students to match learning styles and preferences with the assignment. If all assignments are writing assignments, for example, students who are hands-on or visual learners are at a disadvantage unrelated to the content base itself.

2) <u>Cooperative learning.</u> Cooperative learning activities allow students to share ideas, expertise, and insights within a nonthreatening setting. The focus tends to remain on positive learning rather than on competition.

3) <u>Structured environment.</u> Some students need and benefit from clear structure which defines the expectations and goals of the teacher. The student knows what is expected and when, and can work and plan accordingly.

4) <u>Clearly stated assignments.</u> Assignments should be clearly stated along with the expectations and criteria for completion. Reinforcement and practice activities should not be a guessing game for the students. The exception to this is, of course, those situations in which a discovery method is used.

5) <u>Independent practice.</u> Independent practice involving application and repetition is necessary for thorough learning. Students learn to be independent learners through practicing independent learning. These activities should always be within the students' abilities to perform successfully without assistance.

6) <u>Repetition.</u> Very little learning is successful with a single exposure. Learners generally require multiple exposures to the same information for learning to take place. However, this repetition does not have to be dull and monotonous. In conjunction with #1 above, varied assignments can provide repetition of content or skill practice without repetition of specific activities. This helps keep learning fresh and exciting for the student.

7) <u>Overlearning.</u> As a principle of effective learning, overlearning recommends that students continue to study and review after they have achieved initial mastery. The use of repetition in the context of varied assignments and activities offers the means to help students pursue and achieve overlearning.

Skill 4. Determine the readability level of instructional materials.

One of the ongoing concerns for teachers is determining whether classroom materials and supplemental materials used in the classroom are appropriate for the age or grade level of the students. This concern has been addressed most frequently through the use of readability formulas which give estimated reading level difficulty. This is, at best, an inexact science. Just as obvious that not all third graders are of similar ability, it is clear that material appropriate for a "typical" third grader will be too difficult for some and quite easy for others.

The reasoning behind the use of readability formulas is that if a method can be used to quantify the difficulty of reading material, the results can be translated to approximations of grade level appropriateness. While such formulas can be helpful, the information so obtained should be considered just one source of data on which to base a decision.

CHARACTERISTICS OF READABILITY FORMULAS

Early readability formulas were quite complex and involved examination of numerous, often varied, factors. Over time, it became apparent that acceptably reliable results could be obtained through greatly simplified procedures. Thus, most of the readability formulas currently used measure two major factors: vocabulary difficulty and grammatical complexity.

Vocabulary. Measures of vocabulary difficulty are founded on developmental considerations. There is the assumption that students' vocabularies become increasingly more powerful as they grow, and that there tends to be substantial commonality among students of the same age in their vocabulary base. Thus, if there is a large proportion of difficult words, the material is more appropriate for older students.

Syntax (grammatical complexity). Measures of grammatical complexity are also founded on developmental considerations. The assumption here is that sentence and higher level language structure becomes more complex as students mature, and the ability to read and understand complex structures is related to age and grade level. The assessment focus for readability formulas is on the sentence level. Sentences with multiple phrases and clauses are presumed to be more difficult to read and comprehend.

USING READABILITY FORMULAS

Most readability formulas are relatively straightforward to use, although some are more time-consuming than others. Typically, the teacher or other user calculates a measure of vocabulary difficulty and a measure of grammatical complexity. The results are then used in a mathematical formula which produces an estimate of readability level. The readability level estimate is almost always in the form of a grade level number.

Passage selection. Most readability formulas require the user to select several passages (often three) at random from the book to be assessed. The length of the passages is based on a specified number of words or sentences. Some guidelines are offered such as selecting a passage from the first third, middle third, and last third of the book. There are usually stipulations such as beginning with the first sentence of a paragraph for each selection. Also, the passages should be complete verbal passages without bullet lists, charts, etc., included.

Vocabulary. Vocabulary estimates are generally intended to determine the frequency or percentage of words which a reader may find to be "difficult" to read. These measures are typically based on one of three procedures.

Procedures for Estimating Vocabulary Difficulty
consulting word lists
counting syllables
counting letters

Some formulas provide words lists of high frequency words or "easy" words. The user compares the words in the text passage to the words on the list. Words which are not on the word list are counted as "difficult" words. Since these word lists sometimes run to one thousand or more words, this can be a tedious procedure. Another method of determining difficult words is to count syllables in words. Those words with more than a predetermined number of syllables (often three) are counted as "difficult" words. A few formulas count letters instead of syllables. Words with more than a predetermined number of letters are counted as "difficult" words.

Grammatical complexity. The complexity of sentence structure is presumed to mirror the complexity of the ideas and relationships presented in the passage. The length of the sentence is generally the basis of assessment. The more words there are in a sentence, the more likely it is to include additional phrases or clauses. There are three common methods of estimating the complexity of the sentences.

Procedures for Estimating Grammatical Complexity
average number of words per sentence
average number of sentences per passage
average number of words per passage

The specific procedure used is often related to the method by which the sample passages are selected (see above). The average number of words per sentence is often calculated when the sample passage is selected based on a specified number of sentences. Alternatively, the number of words per passage is sometimes calculated. The average number of sentences per passage is often calculated when the sample passage is based on a specified number of words.

There are dozens of readability formulas in existence, most of which are adequate for general use. However, even among the more popular formulas, there are differences which make certain formulas more appropriate for specific types or levels of materials. Frequently, the directions for the formula will specify reasonable grade levels or types of reading material to be assessed with that formula. Some of the more commonly used readability formulas are listed below.

Common Readability Formulas
Dale-Chall Readability Formula
Fry's Readability Graph
McLaughlin's SMOG Formula
Raygor Readability Estimate
Rudolf Flesch "Reading Ease" Formula

LIMITATIONS OF READABILITY FORMULAS

As may be obvious by now, there are substantive limitations to readability formulas and their use. These limitations do not necessarily invalidate the formulas, but they do place a responsibility on the user to be cautious regarding the conclusions and generalizations made from the results.

Readability formulas focus almost exclusively on word and sentence complexity and even in this arena provide only estimates of the text difficulty. The fact that the results are not precise measures, but are derived from generalized assumptions about the characteristics of difficult text, is one limitation that must be noted. Further limitations include the inability of such formulas to assess the many non-text factors that influence text difficulty. Several significant factors which contribute to reading comprehension but which are not accounted for by readability formulas are listed here.

Factors Not Assessed by Readability Formulas
the prior knowledge base of the reader
the interest of the reader in the topic
the reader's attitude toward reading
the reader's attitude toward reading this particular book
wide ranging differences in vocabulary makeup among students

Yet it is often these unassessed variables which contribute most significantly to the reader's ability to comprehend a particular reading assignment. Other factors such as cultural and socioeconomic characteristics, frequently have a pronounced, if somewhat indirect, effect on the reader's ability to read and understand a given passage or book. Thus, readability formulas provide important, but incomplete, information about the difficulty of a book and its appropriateness for students of particular ages or grade levels.

Skill 5. Demonstrate the ability to match instructional materials to children's abilities in all content areas.

It is often quite difficult to identify a specific reading level performance for a student which enables a teacher to select or provide reading material appropriate for the student. The difficulty arises from two sources: the challenge to determine and describe the student's reading ability, and the challenge to identify and determine the aspects of a text passage which most strongly affect the difficulty of the material.

When students are asked to read and learn independently from reading materials, most often textbooks, it is imperative that the students have the ability to read and understand the material. Unfortunately, this is frequently not the case. Textbooks are often more difficult than the grade level for which they are intended. Teachers have essentially two options when this is the case. First, the teacher can provide additional scaffolding and prior knowledge instruction to enable the students to handle the material. The second choice is to obtain materials which cover the same content but which are written in a more easily read style.

This leads us to another definition of readability. Readability can be thought of, not just as the difficulty of the material, but as a match between the reader's ability and the difficulty of the material. A standard readability formula makes two basic assumptions which often lead to inappropriate determination of the student's ability to read certain material. First, there is the assumption that an appropriate grade level designation can be determined for the book and, second, there is the assumption that most students in a given grade level will be able to adequately read material so designated.

There are some methods, not based on the use of readability formulas, which can be used to match students to appropriate reading material. The cloze procedure, which has fallen into disfavor as a comprehension assessment procedure, remains a solid approach to matching students and materials. The procedure is easy to use, easy to score, and has a number of desirable characteristics for the classroom teacher. The major limitation of the cloze procedure is that it can be extremely frustrating for the student completing the task. Under standard reading conditions, a comprehension level of less than 70% is considered to be inadequate and to reflect material too difficult for the reader. With the cloze procedure, however, a score of 50% is considered to represent successful comprehension. This discrepancy is the source of much frustration for many readers. Used to comparatively high levels of understanding, they encounter, even in the best of circumstances, a situation which is not, to the student's perception, a successful reading experience.

The cloze procedure remains useful because of the task characteristics which reflect, albeit somewhat indirectly, many factors which readability formulas do not assess. The ability of the reader to supply the specific word for a blank reflects not only the obvious vocabulary base, but awareness of syntax, parts of speech, and the crucial sensitivity to the author's writing style.

There are many sources of guidelines for creating and using cloze passages. The directions are typically quite easy to follow and are well within the capabilities of classroom teachers. For applications intended to match students to reading materials, it is simply a matter of selecting sample passages from the book under consideration and developing the cloze passages accordingly. If your concern is to determine whether the standard classroom textbook is appropriate for your students, administering a few cloze selections from the textbook will provide solid evidence as to whether the class as a whole, and specific individual students, can be reasonably expected to handle the reading assignments or whether they will likely need additional support.

Administering and scoring cloze passages are not complex activities. These passages can be given to the entire class simultaneously, eliminating the need for individualized assessment sessions. Over a period of several days, passages from several source materials may be used to guide decisions for selecting a classroom book or for selecting supplemental materials for certain students. Passages should be scored for exact replacement of the omitted word. While it seems only "fair" to give credit for synonyms, there is little empirical evidence to recommend doing so. First, keep in mind that you are not "grading" these activities as such (they are not appropriate for summative assessments) and therefore the specific score a student receives should not be compared to the percentages used for assigning grades. The reason for scoring these passages is to determine the adequacy of the material. Accepting synonyms will, generally, inflate the scores somewhat, but the rank order among the students remains virtually unchanged. Accepting synonyms voids the standard percentage charts used to determine whether material is appropriate for the reader. The primary drawback to accepting synonyms is that doing so lowers the reliability of the assessment since the scorer's judgement becomes a factor in determining which synonyms are acceptable.

Another procedure which can be used to match readers and materials is an informal reading inventory. While there are a number of commercial informal reading inventories available, these have little direct use in matching materials and readers. It is not too difficult, though, to create your own informal reading inventory using the textbook or other materials of interest as the basis for the passages. The procedures for doing this are less restrictive than those for developing cloze passages. Select passages which most clearly represent the nature and difficulty of the book. The length of the passage may vary according to the age of the students and the topic. As a general rule, keep the passage short enough that the students can read it in two to four minutes.

Then develop five to ten questions based on the reading material. These questions should be passage dependent. You should also include questions at various levels of comprehension (details, inferences, vocabulary, etc.) to provide a cross-section of information. Comprehension rates of 70% and up generally indicate material appropriate for classroom use with some teacher guidance.

Other possibilities include oral reading miscue analysis, interest inventories, attitude surveys, prior knowledge assessments, and student self-appraisal. Each of these procedures provides limited information and the combination of two or more procedures is recommended. The Irwin-Davis Readability Checklist (1980) offers still another approach to matching materials and readers. This checklist guides the teacher through a critique of the key features of the text and provides a procedure to identify potential problem areas (and strength areas) of the reading material.

Skill 6. Use the results of standardized, commercial, and teacher-made tests in classroom instruction.

Tests have evolved as an integral component of educational assessment. Keep in mind, though, that tests comprise only a portion of the assessment procedures and information employed by the classroom teacher. Tests can serve a variety of educational purposes in the classroom. They may provide information for placement in leveled materials, for grouping decisions, for diagnostic purposes, for formative instructional decisions, and for summative assessments.

Standardized tests have been formed (or standardized) on large populations and provide various kinds of comparative information. This information generally describes average performance levels for students of particular grade levels, ages, geographical areas, school sizes, socioeconomic characteristics, and other population characteristics. These tests are usually available on a national basis and include most of the tests known to the general public.

Commercial tests are pre-packaged tests available to the classroom teacher through various avenues. Most commonly, these are the tests that come with publisher-supplied support materials for specific textbooks or instructional material sets. These often include pretests, posttests, placement tests and tests of prior knowledge, in addition to chapter and unit tests.

Teacher-made tests are those tests created or modified by the teacher for use in the classroom. Many teachers prefer to create their own tests in the belief that they can more directly address the instructional content and thus provide a more valid measure of student learning. The quality of teacher-made tests varies widely depending on the test-writing skill of the individual teacher. Teachers who modify existing publisher-provided tests often develop high quality and appropriate tests for their students.

Test results are often presented in one of two ways. They may be norm-referenced, in which case the results make comparisons to other test-takers. Or they may be criterion-referenced, in which each student's performance is compared to a standard (or criterion) of performance. This distinction is crucial in order for the teacher to clearly understand just what the test results tell about a student or students.

Norm-referenced tests generally report scores in terms of:
> --percentiles
> --quartiles
> --stanines

Criterion-referenced tests generally report scores in terms of:
> --percentages
> --grade level equivalents (GLE)
> --raw scores
> --pass/fail
> --letter grades

One popular advantage of tests is that they provide data which is easily quantifiable and thus make comparisons of students and groups appear to be easy. But it is often this very desire to compare students, groups, and schools which leads to concerns about the role of testing in education. The risk in making these comparisons lies primarily in concerns with the validity and generalizability of the test results. A standardized test, which is designed for purposes of comparison, is not likely to clearly assess the actual classroom instruction experienced by the students. Thus, standardized tests should not be used to assign grades. Standardized tests often provide valuable information for diagnostic purposes and for purposes of grouping students for instruction, especially at the beginning of the school year when the classroom teacher has few objective sources of information concerning the students.

The results of tests are often considered when making instructional decisions and adjustments. When tests are used for grouping decisions, the groups are invariably based on ability as measured by the test. While this may be an appropriate starting point, a student's membership in any group should be viewed as flexible and tentative. It is quite likely that a few students in any given classroom will be assigned to an inappropriate group on the basis of testing alone. The test results should not take primacy over the teacher's professional judgement and observations.

When tests are used to assign grades, the tests must clearly assess the material that was presented to the students. A publisher-supplied test, for example, may test the same information as was taught, but may place substantially more or less emphasis on certain components than did the teacher.

Some publisher-provided tests have been shown to be of questionable quality, although many such tests are quite adequate. If the classroom instruction has closely followed the information presented in the textbook and related materials, the supplied test may be quite reasonable for assessment of student learning. Due to the many variables involved in classroom instruction, however, these tests should not be used to make comparisons among students and groups.

Teacher-made tests can potentially provide the greatest accuracy of assessment. But, as noted above, the quality of the test is directly related to the teacher's expertise in constructing tests. The more carefully a test is constructed to provide an accurate assessment of a particular class or group of students, the less generalizable the results will be. Thus, teacher-made tests are not appropriate instruments for comparisons among classrooms and larger groups.

Skill 7. Demonstrate the ability to construct tests to measure students' performances, based on objectives taught.

Perhaps the most important caveat in creating and using tests for classroom purposes is the old adage to "test what you teach". In perhaps a more planful approach, it is better stated that you should "teach what you plan to test". This second phrasing more clearly reflects the need for thorough planning of the entire instructional program. Before you begin instruction, you should have the assessment planned and defined.

The first step, then, in constructing a classroom test is to establish clear objectives for the instruction. Once the objectives are clearly defined, then it is necessary to assure that those objectives are taught to the students. The test should be viewed as continuation of the instructional process, not as an isolated element that comes at the end.

One common method of matching the test to the instruction is to develop a Table of Specifications. A Table of Specifications is a two-way grid in which the objectives of instruction are listed on one axis and the content which has been presented is listed on the other axis. Then the individual cells are assigned percentages which reflect the focus and extent of instruction in each area. The final step is to distribute the number of questions to be used on the test among the cells of the table in proportion to the identified percentages.

The test. There are few hard and fast rules for constructing tests. Every application is unique and may reasonably differ from one another is many aspects. However, there are a number of general characteristics and considerations which offer appropriate guidelines for most applications. The following list may be helpful.

Desirable characteristics of the TEST

1) The heading should include identification of the subject, test, date, and student name.
2) There should be a variety of test item types. Each item type should be grouped together. The easier types of items (e.g. T/F) should come first and the more difficult types of items (e.g. essay) should come last.
3) All directions should be clear and easy to find. Include directions for the test as a whole and specific directions for each item type or section of the test. Be sure to address issues such as guessing, marking answers, and spelling as needed.
4) Pay attention to how you format the test. Use indenting, plenty of white space, and other visual keys to help students complete the test with a minimum of stress.
5) Control the length of the test. This includes both the physical length and the amount of time required to complete the test.

Test items. The type of test item used to assess an objective should be determined by the nature of the information or process of interest. Select the type of item which most directly measures the information desired.

Desirable characteristics of the test ITEMS

True/False. Use direct statements and avoid unattributed opinions. The correct answer should be clearly obvious to knowledgeable individuals.

Multiple Choice. The stem should be an incomplete statement or a question. The answer choices should be grammatically consistent with the stem and should be reasonable responses. Only one answer should be correct.

Matching. The items should share a common characteristic (e.g. dates, historical events, names). Provide more answer choices than items. Keep all on one page. Have young children draw a line between the item and answer to simplify the task.

Fill-in-the-blank. To avoid giving extraneous clues, make all blanks the same length. To avoid giving grammatical clues use "a(n)" and similar constructions before a blank. Use this item type to assess recall of key terms and other factual information.

Short Answer/Essay. Provide adequate space for writing the response. Be certain the directions clearly state what is expected. Identify significant scoring criteria, such as "spelling will count".

Skill 8. Make assignments appropriate for a child's developmental level and family and homelife.

When making assignments for students, particularly homework and other out of class assignments, it is necessary to consider factors other than direct educational concerns. The students differ in terms of attention span, concentration ability, their willingness and ability to complete various types of tasks (such as hands-on or visually based activities, standard paper and pencil tasks, and so forth), and in their ability to independently meet specific performance standards regarding spelling, neatness, and so on.

For a given assignment, the students will require varying amounts of support, encouragement, and assistance from parents or other adults at home. Since many students have non-supportive homelife settings, it is important to keep assignments within the ability of the student to complete with a minimum of adult supervision.

Even in very supportive environments, the teacher must be cognizant of restrictions on the ability of parents or other adults to provide time or materials. Some families may not have easy, quick access to the books, magazines, or newspapers that may be requested for completion of an assignment. Money requests from school for additional supplies, field trips, and similar purposes are also beyond the means of some parents. Similarly, transportation requirements such as a trip to the grocery store or the local library may be difficult for many parents. These factors, and other factors of which you learn, should be considered when planning out-of-class assignments for your students.

Skill 9. Use effective conferencing and communication techniques (oral and written) to inform parents of test results, achievement progress, and classroom behavior.

The support of the parent is an invaluable aid in the educational process. It is in the best interests of child, parent, and teacher for there to be cooperation and mutual support between parent and teacher. One of the teacher's professional responsibilities is to establish and maintain effective communication with parents. A few basic techniques to pursue are oral communication (phone calls), written communication in the form of general information classroom newsletters, notes to the parent of a particular child, and parent-teacher conferences.

Teachers should share with parents items of interest, including but not limited to, classroom rules and policies, class schedules and routines, homework expectations, communication procedures, conferencing plans, and other similar information. Much of this can be done in a newsletter format sent home early in the school year. It is imperative that all such written communications be error free. It is a good idea to have another teacher read your letter before you send it out. Good writing and clear communication are learned skills and require time and effort to develop.

When you find it necessary to communicate (whether by phone, letter, or in person) with a parent regarding a concern about a student, allow yourself a "cooling off" period before making contact with the parent. It is important that you remain professional and objective. Your purpose for contacting the parent is to elicit support and additional information which may have a bearing on the student's behavior or performance. Be careful that you do not demean the child and do not appear antagonistic or confrontational. Be aware that the parent is likely to be quite uncomfortable with the "bad news" and will respond best if you take a cooperative, problem-solving approach to the issue. It is also a nice courtesy to notify parents of positive occurrences with their children. The teacher's communication with parents should not be limited to negative items.

PARENT CONFERENCES

The parent-teacher conference is generally for one of three purposes. First, the teacher may wish to <u>share information</u> with the parents concerning the performance and behavior of the child. Second, the teacher may be interested in <u>obtaining information</u> from the parents about the child. Such information may help answer questions or concerns which the teacher has. A third purpose may be to <u>request parent support</u> or involvement in specific activities or requirements. In many situations, more than one of the purposes may be involved.

<u>Planning the conference.</u> When a conference is scheduled, whether at the request of the teacher or the parent, the teacher should allow sufficient time to prepare thoroughly. Collect all relevant information, samples of student work, records of behavior, and other items needed to help the parent understand the circumstances. It also a good idea to compile a list of questions or concerns you wish to address. Arrange the time and location of the conference to provide privacy and to avoid interruptions.

<u>Conducting the conference.</u> Begin the conference by putting the parents at ease. Take the time to establish a comfortable mood, but do not waste time with unnecessary small talk. Begin your discussion with positive comments about the student. Identify strengths and desirable attributes, but do not exaggerate.

As you address issues or areas of concern, be sure to focus on observable behaviors and concrete results or information. Do not make judgmental statements about parent or child. Share specific work samples, anecdotal records of behavior, etc., which demonstrate clearly the concerns you have. Be a good listener and hear the parent's comments or explanations. Such background information can be invaluable in understanding the needs and motivations of the child.

Finally, end the conference with an agreed plan of action between parents and teacher (and, when appropriate, the child). Bring the conference to a close politely but firmly and thank the parents for their involvement.

<u>After the conference.</u> A day or two after the conference, it is a good idea to send a follow-up note to the parents. In this note, briefly and concisely reiterate the plan or steps agreed to in the conference. Be polite and professional; avoid the temptation to be too informal or chatty. If the issue is a long term one such as the behavior or on-going work performance of the student, make periodic follow-up contacts to keep the parents informed of the progress.

COMPETENCY 25.0 Establishes a testing environment in which students can validly demonstrate their knowledge and/or skill, and receive adequate information about the quality of their test performance

SKILL 25.1 Demonstrates effective procedures for orienting students to tests, specifying test content and instructing students in test-taking prior to administration of a test.

Tests are essential instructional tools. They can greatly influence students' learning and should not be taken lightly nor given without due regard for the importance of preparation. Several studies have been carried out which indicate conclusively that students perform better when they understand what type of test they are going to take and why they are taking the test before they take the test.

If students perceive a test to be important or to have relative significance, they will perform better. In a recent study, students who were informed by their teachers as to how their test scores were to be used and who were also urged by their teachers to put forth their best effort scored higher on the Differential Aptitudes Test than students who did not receive this coaching.

It is a recognized fact that students will attain higher test scores if they are familiar with the format of the test. It is important for the student to know whether he/she will be taking a multiple choice test or an essay test. Being prepared for a specific test format can enhance test scores.

Teachers can help students boost their test performance by providing them with explicit information in regard to the content of the test.

SKILL 25.2 Administers tests in ways to reduce debilitating anxiety discourage cheating, and control potential distractions

It is important to be aware of the effects that anxiety can have upon test outcomes. Anxiety can undermine a student's test performance and can actually be induced by the examiner. Stressing the importance of a test or implying that achievement may be conditional based upon test scores just prior to administering a test may cause great anxiety and be detrimental to test scores. In simple terms, students should not be intimidated by an impending test nor threatened with dire consequences if they do not do well on a test.

Anxiety may begin in the classroom and may only increase as a testing situation approaches. In 1985, S. Zatz and L. Chassin did a study comparing classroom environments and test results. In classrooms which students perceived as being threatening, high test anxiety existed and was associated with poor test performance although the students were high achievers. A high threat classroom was defined as "one in which there was a perceived emphasis on academic competition and the teacher was perceived as enforcing rules strictly and punishing infractions severely." (FPMS Domains,1991) No relationship was found to exist between classroom environment and student test performance in "low threat classrooms". (PMS Domains, 1991) Teachers should attempt to create a non-threatening atmosphere in the classroom in order for student learning to occur and for student test scores to increase.

Because of the prevalence of high anxiety, several studies have been conducted to evaluate the relationship between test anxiety and test and classroom performance. These studies have concluded that anxiety has had a negative effect on test-taking and on test scores. It was found that even students who were well prepared for and who had studied sufficiently for a test scored poorly due to test anxiety. Students with good test-taking skills and high anxiety scored poorly on tests as compared to students with weak test-taking skills and low anxiety. Students with both poor skills and high anxiety had the lowest test scores regardless of their ability or aptitude.

The testing environment can have both negative and positive effects on test scores. The teacher must make physical arrangements which contribute to student performance on tests. These arrangements include comfortable seating, adequate lighting, appropriate room temperature, and proper ventilation. Although the physical setting is important, studies have shown that students will be able to tolerate less than ideal physical settings without serious consequences.

It is somewhat important to control, or at least limit, outside distractions especially among younger children. It was determined in a study of two groups of fifth grade students that repeated disturbances resulted in lower test scores. In a similar study, high school students were interrupted by a trumpeter, someone entering the classroom talking, loud whispering, arguing occurring outside the classroom, and mistiming of the test, however they scored as well as the students in the control group. It was concluded that with older students commonly occurring distractions do not effect test results.

The implications of cheating are many. One of the greatest concerns to the teacher is the validity of test scores if cheating has occurred. Therefore, teachers may find it necessary to take precautions to reduce the incidence of cheating. Effective procedures to control cheating include: providing ample advance notice of an upcoming test, spending sufficient class time preparing for a test, using an original test, planning seating arrangements, providing close supervision and acknowledging and enforcing consequences for cheating.

Several studies were carried out in the 1960's to determine the incidence, causes, and repercussions of cheating. It was found that teacher personality and teaching style had a definite correlation to cheating.

Teachers who were very authoritarian and/or totalitarian seemed to have more serious problems with students cheating than teachers who were more democratic and/or reasonable. It was also found that situational factors contributed more significantly to cheating than student behavioral factors. These situational factors included the teacher leaving the classroom during testing, the emotional tone of the classroom, and the moral climate of the school. According to these studies the rate of the incidence of cheating varies but at any given time approximately 35% of the students cheat on tests. As previously stated, cheating is detrimental to test validity and can have a negative impact on both teaching and, more importantly, learning. in 1990, E. D. Evans and D. Craig administered a questionnaire to more than 1,500 students and over 100 teachers. Both teachers and students admitted that cheating occurs and is a problem. Students considered cheating to be a more serious problem than teachers did and expressed that perhaps teachers were not aware of the magnitude of the incidence of cheating. Students admitted that they frequently know who is cheating and when cheating occurs but that they usually do not report the cheating to the teacher nor complain about the cheating to the students who are cheating. Students in this study indicated that teacher characteristics and behaviors contributed to cheating. They agreed that "unfriendly, boring teachers who have unrealistically high expectations for student performance are more likely to encounter cheating. Both students and teachers also agreed that teachers who don't take steps to prevent cheating are likely to encounter it." (FPMS Domains, 1990)

SKILL 25.3 Provides feedback on test results in a manner which expresses approval and gives information for correcting errors in understanding.

When teachers provide feedback to students on their tests, motivation, learning and retention of knowledge will increase. During a feedback session, the teacher should allow the students to explain their answers and use this opportunity to clarify misconceptions. Many teachable moments will naturally arise from students' questions and time should be allocated for open discussion and questioning. Students will gain pertinent information from classmates as well as from the teacher which will facilitate correcting errors in understanding. Effective teachers realize that a test is not a culminating activity but rather a starting point for instruction and a critical aspect of the learning cycle.

For the greatest retention of knowledge or skills to be attained, the timing of feedback is important. In many cases immediate feedback is not as effective as delayed feedback. According to research, it is better for feedback to occur at least 24 hours after testing. Often, if feedback is immediate, the student is likely to remember the answer that they gave even if it was incorrect. When feedback is delayed by a couple of days, learners perform better on a retest.

COMPETENCY 26.0 Utilizes an effective system for maintaining records of student and class progress.

SKILL 26.1 Constructs a system for recording the progress of individual students and the total class.

Many tools are available for establishing records of student progress. One of the essential tools for recording student progress is the teacher grade book in which the teacher enters the grades of each student in each content area. These grades can later be transposed onto other forms or into other records when necessary. Currently, teacher grade books are the official document which reflect student progress.

Sometimes teachers will utilize a chart which can give a global picture of both a student's progress and also the progress of the total class. Such a chart can be beneficial to the teacher in assessing at a glance which students are on target and which students may need additional help or direction. These charts also provide the teacher with a comparative viewpoint of all students.

When teachers record the progress that students are making with specific skills, a check list can be used. This form contains a list of skills pertaining to a particular content area. Teachers can indicate if the student is making satisfactory progress, needs more instruction, or has mastered any or all of the skills listed. This type of check list gives a good picture of the students' strengths and weaknesses.

An efficient means of showing student progress is through the use of student portfolios. In a portfolio, the student keeps a collection of dated samples of his/her work over a period of time. The teacher can discuss the contents of the student's portfolio with the student giving feedback as to areas of concern and how to make improvements. The teacher can also discuss with the student those aspects of the student's work that the student believes are accurate reflections of the student's best work. From time to time, the teacher will ask the student to select a sample of quality work to be included in a teacher's class portfolio. By comparing the works from the beginning of the school year with later assignments, the teacher, student, and others can clearly see the student's progress.

Teachers may make anecdotal records of a student's progress. Anecdotal records include both global and behavioral observations made by the teacher. Anecdotal records are dated, informal notations that describe language development as well as social development in terms of the learner's attitudes, strengths, weaknesses, needs, progress, learning styles, skills, strategies used, or anything else that seems significant at the time of the observation. These records are usually brief comments that are very specific to what the child is doing and needs to be doing. They provide documented, accumulated information.

SKILL 26. 2 Identifies effective methods for reporting individual student and class progress.

The most widely used method for reporting individual student progress is the traditional report card. Report cards are still viewed as legal documentation of a student's academic standing. Report cards include grade averages for each content area as well as a record of student attendance. Most report cards have a section that denotes the student's behavior. The majority of the parents prefer the report card to other forms of evaluation because they are most familiar with it.

One of the most effective means of reporting student progress is the parent/teacher conference. Many schools require at least one parent/teacher conference each year. A conference is a face to face meeting between parents and the teacher. Sometimes students may also attend a conference. Conferences give teachers the opportunity to discuss students' behaviors and accomplishments. Parents can get clarification on questions that they have regarding the student's progress and can receive information about how they can help their child. Student's work samples and goals can be discussed. Most importantly, parents have the opportunity to give input as to their child's academic program and progress expectations.

Teachers may incorporate the narrative report approach. Due to conflicting schedules, parents cannot always come to the school but they would like to receive more information than the standard report card gives. At such times, the teacher can give a written narrative of the student's strengths and weaknesses, behaviors, attitudes and academic progress. Narrative reports are usually rather informal as compared to the report card and serve as a means of one way communication from the school to the home.

SKILL 26.3 Demonstrates knowledge of the contents and procedures for maintaining student permanent records.

The student permanent record is a file of the student's cumulative educational history. It contains a profile of the student's academic background as well as the student's behavioral and medical background. Other pertinent individual information contained in the permanent record includes the student's attendance, grade averages, and schools attended. Personal information such as parents' names and addresses, immunization records, child's height and weight, and narrative information about the child's progress and physical and mental well-being is an important aspect of the permanent record. All information contained within the permanent record is strictly confidential and is only to be discussed with the student's parents or other involved school personnel.

The purpose of the permanent record is to provide applicable information about the student so that the student's individual educational needs can be met. If any specialized testing has been administered, the results are noted in the permanent record. Any special requirements that the student may have are indicated in the permanent record. Highly personal information including court orders regarding custody are filed in the permanent record as is appropriate. The importance and value of the permanent record cannot be underestimated. It offers a comprehensive knowledge of the student.

The current teacher is responsible for maintaining the student's permanent record. All substantive information in regard to testing, academic performance, the student's medical condition, and personal events are placed in the permanent record file. Updated information in regard to the student's grades, attendance, and behavior is added annually. These files are kept in a locked fireproof room or file cabinet and cannot be removed from this room unless the person removing them signs a form acknowledging full responsibility for the safe return of the complete file. Again, only the student's parents (or legal guardians), the teacher or other concerned school personnel may view the contents of the permanent record file.

The permanent record file follows the student as he/she moves through the school system with information being updated along the way. Anytime the student leaves a school, the permanent record is transferred with the student. The permanent record is regarded as legal documentation of a student's educational experience.

SKILL 26.4 Demonstrates knowledge of the laws and policies governing the content and use of student records.

The contents of any student records should be indicative of the student's academic aptitude and/or achievement. The information contained should never be in any way derogatory or potentially damaging. It is important to keep in mind that others who view the contents of the records may form an opinion of the student based on the information in the student's record or file. Anyone who places information in a student's record must make every effort to give an accurate reflection of the student's performance while maintaining a neutral position as to the student's potential for future success or failure.

The most essential fact to remember in regard to students' records is that the information within is confidential. Although specific policies may vary from one school or district to another, confidentiality remains constant and universal. Teachers never discuss any student or his/her progress with anyone other than the student's parents or essential school personnel. Confidentiality applies to all student information whether it is a student's spelling test, portfolio, standardized test information, report card, or the contents of the permanent record file.

The significance of the student's records is not to be taken lightly. In many instances, teachers have access to a student's records before she actually meets the student. It is important for the teacher to have helpful information about the student without developing any preconceived biases about the student. Careful regard must be given to all information that is added to a student's file without diluting the potential effectiveness of that information. It is also important to be cognizant of the fact that the primary function of the student records is that it is intended to be used as a means of developing a better understanding of the student's needs and to generate a more effective plan for meeting these needs.

SKILL 26.5 Recognizes the ethical and legal impacts and consequences of a computerized society.

In this technological age, it is important that teachers be aware of their legal responsibilities when using computers in the classroom. As public employees, teachers are particularly vulnerable to public scrutiny. Not only are teachers more likely to be caught if they are unethical in the use of computers in the classroom but it is also the responsibility of educators to model as well as teach ethical computer behaviors.

In 1980, P.L. 96-517, Section 117 of the copyright was amended to cover the use of computers. The following changes were made:

1. The definition of a "computer program" was inserted and is defined now as "a set of statements or instructions to be used directly in a computer in order to bring about a certain result."

2. The Owner of a copy of a computer program is not infringing on the copyright by making or authorizing the making of or adaptation of that program if the following criteria are met:

    a. The new copy or adaptation must be created in order to be able to use the program in conjunction with the machine and is used in no other manner.

    b. The new copy or adaptation must be for archival purpose only and all archival copies must be destroyed in the event that continued possession of the computer program should cease to be rightful.

    c. Any copies prepared or adapted may not be leased, sold, or otherwise transferred without the authorization of the copyright owner.

The intent of this amendment to the copyright act is to allow an individual or institutional owner of a program to make "backup" copies to avoid destruction of the original program disk, while restricting the owner from making copies in order to use the program on more that one machine at a time or to share with other teachers. Under the Software Copyright Act of 1980, once a program is loaded into the memory of a computer, a temporary copy of that program is made. Multiple machine loading (moving from machine to machine and loading a single program into several computers for simultaneous use) constitutes making multiple copies which is not permitted under the law. Since the same is true of a networked program, it is necessary to obtain permission from the owner of the copyright or purchase a license agreement prior to multiple use of a program in a school setting.

Infringement of copyright laws is a serious offense and can result in significant penalties if a teacher chooses to ignore the law. Not only does the teacher risk losing all personal computer equipment but he or she is also placing their job as an educator in jeopardy.

COMPETENCY 27.0 Uses computers in education.

Skill 27.1 Recognizes proper operational procedures for computers.

To a novice, computers might appear to be very complicated machines, but in reality it is not very difficult to operate one of today's "user-friendly" computers. Basically, all that is required is to attach the computer to the power source and turn it on. Most machines are configured to "boot up" into a menu of programs from which the user has merely to "point and click" at the desired choice.

For the computer to boot up from the hard drive to follow the instructions for which it has been configured, it is necessary to remove any diskettes from the floppy disk drive before turning on the power. Otherwise, the computer will not boot up into its menu from the hard drive, but rather will try to find the necessary boot up instructions on the floppy disk.

When preparing to shut down the computer, it is important to close all programs that are currently in use. This includes saving anything that needs to be kept for future sessions on the computer. When a program is not properly exited, important data might be lost and the computer might not boot up to the proper menu next time it is turned on. It is just a matter of good housekeeping to put away everything in its proper place before leaving. If the program was accessed from a DOS prompt or menu, the computer should be returned to the same starting place before turning off the machine. Programs accessed from Windows should be exited, all windows should be closed, and Windows itself should be exited by selecting File Exit before the power is turned off. Macintosh computers are much like Windows in that all programs should be exited and all windows closed before choosing SYSTEM and SHUT DOWN. Once everything is properly closed, the computer will give the user a message ["It is safe to turn off your computer"] and the computer can be turned off.

Skill 27.2 Identifies major components and their functions of a computer system commonly used in an educational setting.

The computer system can be divided into 2 main parts - the hardware and the software. Hardware can be defined as all the physical components that make up the machine. Software includes the programs (sets of instructions) that enable that machine to do a particular job.

HARDWARE:

Input devices are those parts of the computer that accept information from the user. The most common input devices are the keyboard and the mouse. Other more specialized input devices might include joysticks, light pens, touch pads, graphic tablets, voice recognition devices, and optical scanners.

Output devices are the parts of the computer that display the results of processing for the user. These commonly include the monitor and printers but a computer might also output information to plotters and speech synthesizers. Monitors and printers can vary greatly in the quality of the output displayed. Monitors are classified according to their resolution (dpi = dots per square inch). SVGA (Super Video Graphics Adapter) monitors are able to display a three dimensional picture that looks almost real. Printers vary in the way they produce "hardcopy" as well as in the quality of the resultant product. Dot matrix printers are the cheapest printers and form an image on the paper by actually impacting the paper much the way a typewriter does. Because the image is composed of dots on the paper, it is not considered "letter" quality, but is usually sufficient for classroom use. Ink jet printers are more expensive both to purchase and to maintain, but because they produce a much clearer image, they are often preferred when the quality of the hardcopy is important. With market prices coming down, they are becoming much more affordable. The best hardcopies are produced by laser printers, but laser printers are also the most expensive. They are usually found in offices where volume is not high but the best quality is desired.

Storage devices enable computers to save documents and other important files for future editing. Hard drives are built into most computers for the storage of the large programs used today. As programs increase in size and complexity to make use of the enhanced graphic and sound capabilities of today's computers, the amount of storage space on a hard drive has become increasingly important. Many schools avoid the limitations imposed by the hard drive's storage space by using networks to deliver programs to the individual systems. Floppy disk drives allow the individual users of a computer system to save personal data and files on portable diskettes that can be carried from one computer to another. The CD ROM drives of multimedia computers that can access CD ROM disks containing large amounts of information and usually including sound, graphics and even video clips.

The last hardware component of a computer system is the Central Processing Unit or CPU along with all the memory chips on the mother board. This "brain" of the computer is responsible for receiving input from the input or storage devices, placing it in temporary storage (RAM or Random Access Memory), performing any processing functions required by the program (like mathematical equations or sorting), and eventually retrieving the information from storage and displaying it by means of an output device.

SOFTWARE Software consists of all the programs containing instructions for the computer and is stored on the hard drive, floppy disks, or CD ROM disks. Programs fall into two major groups - operating system and application programs. Operating system programs contain instructions that allow the computer to function. Applications are all the jobs that a user might wish to perform on the computer. These might include word processors, data bases, spreadsheets, educational and financial programs, games, and telecommunications programs.

Skill 27.3 **Recognizes criteria for selecting software for use in an** **instructional**

setting.

With a surplus of educational software on the market, it is important for an educator to be able to evaluate a program before purchasing it. Software can vary greatly in content, presentation, skill level, and objectives and it is not always possible to believe everything that is advertised on the package. If a teacher is in the position of having to purchase a computer program for use in the classroom without any prior knowledge of the program itself, it is useful to have some guidelines to follow. Once a program has been purchased and the shrink-wrap has been removed, many vendors are reluctant to allow its return because of a possible violation of copyright laws or damage to the software medium. For this reason it is important to preview the software personally before buying it. If a vendor is reluctant to allow the teacher to preview a program prior to its purchase, it is sometimes possible to get a preview copy from the publisher.

Many school districts have addressed this problem by publishing a list of approved software titles for each grade level in much the same way that they publish lists of approved text books and other classroom materials. In addition, most districts have developed a software evaluation form to be used by any instructor involved in the purchase of software that is not already on the "approved" list. Use of a software evaluation form can eliminate a lot of the risk involved when shopping for appropriate titles for the classroom. In many districts, all software is evaluated by the actual instructors that will use the software and the completed evaluation forms are made available for the perusal of other prospective buyers.

The first thing that must be considered before purchasing software is its compatibility with the computer on which it is to be used. If the program will not run efficiently on the computer in the classroom because of hardware limitations, there is no need to continue the evaluation process. Some of the restrictions to consider are the operating system (MS-DOS, Windows, or MacIntosh) for which the particular software package was developed, the recommended memory size, the required hard drive space, the medium type (floppy disk or CD-ROM), the type of monitor, and the need for any special input devices such as a mouse, joystick, or speech card. If a network is used in the classroom or school for which the program is to be purchased, it is also important to know if the program is networkable. Often, programs with a lot of graphics encounter difficulties when accessed from a network.

There are three general steps to follow when evaluating a software program. First one must read the instructions thoroughly to familiarize oneself with the program, its hardware requirements, and its installation. Once the program is installed and ready to run, the evaluator should first run the program as it would be run by a successful student without deliberate errors but making use of all the possibilities available to the student. Thirdly, the program should be run making deliberate mistakes to test the handling of errors. One should try to make as many different kinds of mistakes as possible, including those for incorrect keyboard usage and the validity of user directions.

Most software evaluation forms include the same types of information. There is usually a section for a general description of the program consisting of the intended grade level, additional support materials available, the type of program (game, simulation, drill, etc), stated goals and objectives, and the clarity of instructions. Other sections will provide checklists for educational content, presentation, and type and quality of user interaction with the program.

Once a software package has been thoroughly tested, the teacher will be able to make an intelligent decision regarding its purchase.

Skill 27.4 Recognizes the ethical and legal impacts and consequences of a computerized society.

In this technological age, it is important that teachers be aware of their legal responsibilities when using computers in the classroom. As public employees, teachers are particularly vulnerable to public scrutiny. Not only are teachers more likely to be caught if they are unethical in the use of computers in the classroom but it is also the responsibility of educators to model as well as teach ethical computer behaviors.

In 1980, P.L. 96-517, Section 117 of the copyright was amended to cover the use of computers. The following changes were made:

1. The definition of a "computer program" was inserted and is defined now as "a set of statements or instructions to be used directly in a computer in order to bring about a certain result."

2. The Owner of a copy of a computer program is not infringing on the copyright by making or authorizing the making of another copy or adaptation of that program **IF** the following criteria are met:

    a. The new copy or adaptation must be created in order to be able to use the program in conjunction with the machine and is used in **no other manner**

    b. The new copy or adaptation must be for archival purpose only and all archival copies must be destroyed in the event that continued possession of the computer program should cease to be rightful.

    c. Any copies prepared or adapted may not be leased, sold, or otherwise transferred without the authorization of the copyright owner.

The intent of this amendment to the copyright act is to allow an individual or institutional owner of a program to make "backup" copies to avoid destruction of the original program disk, while restricting the owner from making copies in order to use the program on more that one machine at a time or to share with other teachers. Under the Software Copyright Act of 1980, once a program is loaded into the memory of a computer, a temporary copy of that program is made. Multiple machine loading (moving from machine to machine and loading a single program into several computers for simultaneous use) constitutes making multiple copies which is not permitted under the law. Since the same is true of a networked program, it is necessary to obtain permission from the owner of the copyright or purchase a license agreement prior to multiple use of a program in a school setting.

Infringement of copyright laws is a serious offense and can result in significant penalties if a teacher chooses to ignore the law. Not only does the teacher risk loosing all personal computer equipment but he or she is also placing their job as an educator in jeopardy.

SKILL 27.5 Identifies appropriate school and classroom management applications of computers.

When dealing with large class sizes and at the same time trying to offer opportunities for students to use computers, it is often necessary to use a lot of ingenuity. If the number of computers available for student use is limited, the teacher must take a tip from elementary school teachers who are skilled at managing centers. Students can be rotated singly or in small groups to the computer centers as long as they are well oriented in advance to the task to be accomplished and with the rules to be observed. Rules for using the computer should be emphasized with the whole class prior to individual computer usage in advance and then prominently posted.

If a computer lab is available for use by the curriculum teacher, the problem of how to give each student the opportunity to use the computer as an educational tool might be alleviated, but a whole new set of problems must be dealt with. Again the rules to be observed in the computer lab should be discussed before the class ever enters the lab and students should have a thorough understanding of the assignment. When a large group of students is visiting a computer lab, it is very easy for the expensive hardware to suffer from accidental or deliberate harm if the teacher is not aware of what is going on at all times. Students need to be aware of the consequences for not following the rules because it is so tempting to experiment and show off to their peers.

Unfortunately, students who have access to computers outside of school often feel like they know everything already and are reluctant to listen to instruction on lab etiquette or program usage. The teacher must be constantly on guard to prevent physical damage to the machines from foreign objects finding their way into disk drives, key caps from disappearing from keyboards (or being rearranged), or stray pencil or pen marks from appearing on computer systems. Experienced students also get a lot of enjoyment from saving games on hard drives, moving files into new directories or eliminating them altogether, creating passwords to prevent others from using machines, etc. At the same time the other students need a lot of assistance to prevent accidents caused by their inexperience . It is possible to pair inexperienced students with more capable ones to alleviate some of the problem. Teachers must constantly rotate around the room and students must be prepared before their arrival in the lab so that they know exactly what to do when they get there to prevent them from exercising their creativity.

SKILL 27.6 Selects methods of integrating computers in instruction

There are a lot of computer programs available to enhance instruction in various curricula areas. Tutorials and educational programs and games exist in almost every imaginable subject, but computers can also be used as a tool to enhance regular instruction.

One way to take advantage of the computer's ability to store vast amounts of data is to utilize them in the classroom is as a research tool. Entire encyclopedias, whole classical libraries, specialized databases in history, science, and the arts can be obtained on CD ROM disks to allow students to complete their research from the classroom computer. With the "Search" feature of these programs, students can type in a one or two word description of the desired topic and the computer will actually locate all articles that deal with that topic. The student can either read the articles on the computer monitor or print them out. If the classroom computer has Internet access, the research possibilities are unlimited. When hooked up to the World Wide Web, students can actually talk to people from other parts of the globe or access libraries and journals from all over the world. For example, if students are studying weather, they might go online with students who live in different weather zones to discuss how weather affects their lives. Then they might access global weather reports and print out weather maps, and discuss their research with meteorologists - and all from a single computer station.

Once the research is completed, use of a desktop publishing program on the computer can produce professional quality documents enhanced by typed text, graphs, clip art, and even photos downloaded from the World Wide Web. Even primary grade students can use the computer to type and illustrate their stories on simple publishing programs like the Children's Writing and Publishing Center by The Learning Company. Spell Check programs and other tools included in these publishing programs can assist students in producing top quality work.

The computer should not replace traditional research and writing skills taught to school-age children, but use of the computer as a tool must also be taught to children who live in a technological society. Computers are as much a part of a child's life today as pencils and paper and the capabilities of computers need to be thoroughly explored to enable students to see computers as much more than a glorified "game machine." A major goal of education is to prepare students for their futures in business and the work place and if they are not taught how to use the available technology to its fullest advantage, educators will have failed in at least part of that purpose.

PROFESSIONAL KNOWLEDGE EXAM

1. **What are critical elements of instructional process?**

   A. content, goals, teacher needs

   B. means of getting money to regulate instruction

   C. content, materials, activities, goals, learner needs

   D. materials, definitions, assign-ments

2. **What would improve planning for instruction?**

   A. describe the role of the teacher and student

   B. evaluate the outcomes of instruction

   C. rearrange the order of activities

   D. give outside assignments

3. **When are students more likely to understand complex ideas?**

   A. if they do outside research before coming to class

   B. later when they write out the definitions of complex words

   C. when they attend a lecture on the subject

   D. when they are clearly defined by the teacher and are given examples and nonexamples of the concept

4. **What is one component of the instructional planning model that must be given careful evaluation?**

   A. students' prior knowledge and skills

   B. the script the teacher will use in instruction

   C. future lesson plans

   D. parent participation

5. **When is utilization of instructional materials most effective?**

   A. the activities are sequenced

   B. the materials are prepared ahead of time

   C. the students choose the pages to work on

   D. the students create the instruc-tional materials

6. **What is evaluation of the instruc-tional activity based on?**

   A. student grades

   B. teacher evaluation

   C. student participation

   D. specified criteria

7. **What should a teacher do when students have not responded well to an instructional activity?**

   A. reevaluate learner needs

   B. request administrative help

   C. continue with the activity another day

   D. assign homework on the concept

8. **How can student misconduct be redirected at times?**

   A. the teacher threatens the students

   B. the teacher assigns detention to the whole class

   C. the teacher stops the activity and stares at the students

   D. the teacher effectively handles changing from one activity to another

9. **What is one way of effectively managing student conduct?**

   A. state expectations about behavior

   B. let students discipline their peers

   C. let minor infractions of the rules go unnoticed

   D. increase disapproving remarks

10. **Which of the following increases appropriate behavior more than 80%?**

    A. monitoring the halls

    B. having class rules

    C. having class rules, giving feedback, and having individual consequences

    D. having class rules, and giving feedback

11. **To meet the needs of the student, in which areas of developmental patterns and individual differences is information sought?**

    A. academic, regional, and family background

    B. social, physical, academic bakground

    C. academic, physical, and family background

    D. physical, family, ethnic background

12. **According to Piaget, what stage is characterized by the ability to think abstractly and to use logic?**

    A. concrete operations

    B. pre-operational

    C. formal operations

    D. conservative operational

13. At approximately what age is the average child able to define abstract terms such as honesty and justice?

   A. 10-12 years old

   B. 4-6 years old

   C. 14-16 years old

   D. 6-8 years old

14. According to Piaget's theory of cognitive development, what is the process of incorporating new objects, information or experiences into the existing cognitive structures?

   A. attachment

   B. conservation

   C. Identification

   D. assimilation

15. According to Kohlberg what is the first level of moral development in which judgements are made on the basis of physical consequences and personal needs?

   A. anxiety level

   B. pre-conventional level

   C. post-conventional level

   D. symbolic level

16. Johnny, a middle-schooler, comes to class, uncharacteristically tired, distracted, withdrawn, sullen, and cries easily. What would be the first response made?

   A. send him to the office to sit

   B. call his parents

   C. ask him what is wrong

   D. ignore his behavior

17. Sam, a 10 year old fifth grader, has suddenly started to stutter when speaking. What is the most likely speech problem?

   A. a genetic defect

   B. a new habit

   C. evidence of an emotional conflict

   D. an attention-getting device

18. Andy shows up to class abusive and irritable. He is often late, sleeps in class, sometimes slurs his speech, and has an odor of drinking. What is the first intervention to take?

   A. confront him, relying on a trusting relationship you think you have

   B. do a lesson on alcohol abuse, making an example of him

   C. do nothing; it is better to err on the side of failing to identify substance abuse

   D. call administration, avoid conflict, supervise others carefully

19. A 16 year-old girl who has been looking sad writes an essay in which the main protagonist commits suicide. You overheard her talking about suicide. What do you do?

A. Report this immediately to school administration, talk to the girl, letting her know you will talk to her parents about it

B. Report this immediately to HRS, telling only school administration

C. Report this immediately to school administration and make your own report to HRS if required by protocol in your school. - Do nothing else

D. just give the child some extra attention, as it may just be that's all she's looking for

20. You are leading a substance abuse discussion for health class. The students present that marijuana is not harmful to their health. What set of data would refute their claim?

A. it is more carcinogenic than nicotine, lowers resistance to infection, worsens acne, and damages brain cells

B. it damages brain cells, causes behavior changes in prenatally exposed infants, leads to other drug abuse, and causes short-term memory loss

C. it lowers tolerance for frustration, causes eye damage, increases paranoia, and lowers resistance to infection

D. it leads to abusing alcohol lowers white blood cell count, reduces fertility, and causes gout.

21. Jeanne, a bright, attentive student is in first hour English. She is quiet, but very alert in visually scanning the room in random patterns. Her pupils are dilated and she has a slight but noticeable tremor in her hands. She fails to note a cue given from her teacher. At odd moments she will act as if responding to stimuli that aren't there by suddenly changing her gaze. When spoken to directly, she has a limited response, but her teacher has a sense she is not herself. What should the teacher do?

A. ask the student if she is all right, then let it go, as there are not enough signals to be alarmed

B. meet with the student after class to get more information before making a referral

C. send the student to the office to see the health nurse

D. quietly call for administration, carefully not alarming the class or student in question, remaining calm

22. The teacher is working with an individual student. Jane, who is seated at her desk, begins to hit Alan, who sits next to her. The teacher instructs the individual student to keep working, and quietly speaks to Jane. What is the teacher demonstrating?

A. overlap emersion

B. task-desist overlap

C. task-intrusion overlap

D. alternative behavior

23. Marcus is a first grade boy of good developmental attainment. His learning progress is good the first half of the year. He shows no indicators of emotional distress. After the holiday break, he returns much changed. He is quieter, sullen even, tending to play alone. He has moments of tearfulness. Sometimes almost without cause. He avoids contact with adults as often as he can. Even play with his friends has become limited. He has episodes of wetting not seen before, and often wants to sleep in school. What approach is appropriate for this sudden change in behavior?

    A. give him some time to adjust - the holiday break was probably too much fun to come back to school from

    B. report this change immediately to administration - do not call the parents until administration decides a course of action

    C. document his daily behavior carefully as soon as you notice such a change, report to administration next month or so in a meeting

    D. make a courtesy call to the parents to let them know he is not acting himself, being sure to tell them he is not making trouble for others.

24. What have recent studies regarding effective teachers concluded?

    A. effective teachers let students establish rules

    B. effective teachers establish routines by the sixth week of school

    C. effective teachers state their own policies and establish consistent class rules and procedures on the first day of class

    D. effective teachers establish flexible routines

25. While teaching, three students cause separate disruptions. The teacher selects the major one and tells that student to desist. What is the teacher demonstrating?

    A. deviancy spread

    B. correct target desist

    C. alternative behavior

    D. desist major deviance

26. Robert throws a piece of paper across the room. Dennis, sitting next to Robert, bats the piece of paper to the back of the room. The teacher ignores Dennis and reprimands Robert. What is the teacher demonstrating?

    A. deviant disruption

    B. correct target desist

    C. alternative behavior

    D. serious desist

27. **To maintain the flow of events in the classroom, what should an effective teacher do?**

    A. work only in small groups

    B. use only whole class activities

    C. direct attention to content, rather than focusing the class on misbehavior

    D. follow lectures with written assignments

28. **What is most likely to happen when students witness a punitive or angry desist?**

    A. respond with more behavior disruption

    B. all disruptive behavior stops

    C. students align with teacher

    D. behavior stays the same

29. **What is a teacher statement that implies warmth toward and feeling for the children?**

    A. roughness of desist

    B. clarity of desist

    C. approval-focus desist

    D. task-focus desist

30. **Why is it important for a teacher to pose a question before calling on students to answer?**

    A. it helps to manage student conduct

    B. it keeps the students as a group focused on the classwork

    C. it allows students time to collaborate

    D. it gives the teacher time to walk among the students

31. **Which is an example of specific praise?**

    A. "John, you are the only person in class not paying attention."

    B. "William, I thought we agreed that you would turn in all of your homework."

    C. "Robert, you did a good job getting in line. See how it helped us get to music class on time?"

    D. "Class, you did a great job cleaning up the art room."

32. **According to Brophy, what are the characteristics of effective praise?**

    A. is given unobtrusively and quietly

    B. It specifies the particulars of the accomplishment

    C. is more effective when given frequently

    D. is more effective when given to every seventh response

33. **What is one way a teacher can supplement verbal praise?**

   A. Help students evaluate their own performance and supplies self-reinforcement

   B. give verbal praise more frequently

   C. give tangible rewards such as stickers or treats

   D. have students practice giving verbal praise

34. **Reducing off task time and maximizing the amount of time students spend attending to academic tasks is closely related to which of the following?**

   A. using whole class instruction only

   B. business-like behaviors of the teacher

   C. dealing only with major teaching functions

   D. giving students maximum of two minutes to come to order

35. **The concept of efficient use of time includes which of the following?**

   A. daily review, seatwork, and recitation of concepts

   B. lesson initiation, transition, and comprehension check

   C. review, test, review

   D. punctuality, management transition, and wait time avoidance

36. **Brophy and Evertson found strong and consistent positive relationships between which two items?**

   A. controlled interruptions and students in high achieving classes

   B. teachers spending less class time in discussion and higher test scores

   C. social interaction in the classroom and student achievement

   D. student engagement in work and learning gains for second and third grade students

37. **What was the result of studies done in low SES primary classrooms taught by effective teachers?**

   A. more teacher-student interactions and less time in which a child is unoccupied

   B. no pauses between academic tasks

   C. more tasks chosen by the student

   D. more time spent in small group work

38. **What steps are important in the review of subject matter in the classroom?**

   A. a lesson-initiating review, topic summary and a lesson-end review

   B. a preview of the subject matter, an in-depth discussion, and a lesson end review

   C. a rehearsal of the subject matter and a topic summary within the lesson

   D. a short paragraph synopsis of the previous days lesson and a written review at the end of the lesson

39. What is a sample of an academic transition signal?

   A. "How do clouds form?"

   B. "Today we are going to study clouds."

   C. "We have completed the lesson."

   D. "That completes the description of cumulus clouds. Now we will look at the description of cirrus clouds."

40. What is an example of a low order question?

   A. "Why is it important to recycle items in your home?"

   B. "Compare how glass and plastics are recycled."

   C. "What items do we recycle in our county?"

   D. "Explain the important of recycling in our county."

41. The teacher states that the lesson the students will be engaged in will consist of a review of the material from the previous day, a demonstration of the scientific principle of an electronic circuit, and small group work on setting up an electronic circuit with a battery, wire, and a small bulb. What has the teacher demonstrated?

   A. the importance of reviewing

   B. giving the general framework for the lesson to facilitate learning

   C. giving students the opportunity to leave if they are not interested

   D. providing momentum for the lesson

42. Using wait-time has what effect?

   A. gives structure to the class discourse

   B. the teacher tends to ask fewer chain questions, fewer low level questions and more higher level questions

   C. gives the students time to evaluate the response

   D. gives the opportunity for in-depth discussion about the topic

43. What is one benefit of amplifying a student's response?

   A. it helps the student develop a positive self-image

   B. it's helpful to other students who are in the process of learning the reasoning or steps in answering the question

   C. it allows the teacher to cover more

   D. it keeps the information organized

44. A study by Darch and Gersten that examined the effects of positive feedback on the reading performance of seven and eight-year old learning disabled students found which result?

   A. students exhibited more self-esteem

   B. students exhibited more on-task behavior

   C. students were willing to answer more questions

   D. students worked better in small groups

45. **When is optimal benefit reached when handling an incorrect student response?**

    A. when specific praise is used

    B. when the other students are allowed to correct that student

    C. when the student is redirect to a better problem solving approach

    D. when the teacher asks simple questions, provides cues to clarify, or gives assistance for working out the correct response

46. **For seatwork to be effective, what must occur?**

    A. all seatwork is graded immediately

    B. all seatwork should be explained by another student for clarification

    C. the teacher should monitor and provide corrective feedback for seatwork

    D. seatwork should be a review of the previous day's lesson

47. **What are the two types of performance that teaching entails?**

    A. classroom management and questioning techniques

    B. skill-building and analysis of outcomes

    C. interaction with students and manipulation of subject matter

    D. management techniques and levels of questioning

48. **What are the two ways concepts can be taught?**

    A. factually and interpretively

    B. inductively and deductively

    C. conceptually and inductively

    D. analytically and facilitatively

49. **With which child development theorist is the concept of _preformation_ associated?**

    A. Darwin

    B. Leibnez

    C. Wolff

    D. Gesell

50. **In child development, what word indicates the result of the terms _growth_ and _differentiation_?**

    A. adulthood

    B. progress

    C. maturation

    D. evolution

51. **What is thematically connected language that leads to at least one point called?**

    A. scrambled discourse

    B. thematic unit

    C. connected discourse

    D. verbal behavior

52. **What is the effect of vague discourse on the process of instruction?**

    A. increased student achievement

    B. making the operation of teaching confusing to the student

    C. question overload

    D. increased time spent on the content

53. **What is one instructional behavior that indicates to the student what is important in the subject matter to be studied?**

    A. definitions

    B. concepts

    C. choral response

    D. marker expression

54. **Using pro-active expressions and repetition has what effect on students?**

    A. helps student become aware of important elements of content

    B. helps students develop positive self-esteem

    C. helps students tolerate the lecture format of instruction

    D. helps students to complete homework correctly

55. **How can the teacher help students become more work oriented and less disruptive?**

   A. seek their input for content instruction

   B. challenge the students with a task and show genuine enthusiasm for it

   C. use behavior modification techniques with all students

   D. make sure lesson plans are complete for the week

56. **What is an effective way to prepare students for testing?**

   A. minimize the importance of the test

   B. orient the students to the test, telling them of the purpose, how the results will be used and how it is relevant to them

   C. use the same format for every test they are given

   D. have them construct an outline to study from

57. **What did Samson's study on training in test-taking skills conclude?**

   A. there is no correlation between training in test-taking skills and improved student achievement

   B. there is no long term effect of training in test-taking skills

   C. training in test-taking skills does produce improvement in achievement test performance

   D. training in test-taking skills creates more anxiety over test-taking

58. **How will a student have a fair chance to demonstrate what they know on a test?**

   A. the examiner has strictly enforced rules for taking the test

   B. the examiner provides a comfortable setting free of distractions and positively encourages the students

   C. the examiner provides frequent stretch breaks to the students

   D. the examiner stresses the importance of the test to the grade the student will be given

59. **What is an example of formative feedback?**

   A. results of an intelligence test

   B. correcting the tests in small groups

   C. verbal behavior that expresses approval of a student response to a test item

   D. scheduling a discussion prior to the test

60. **How could a KWL chart be used in instruction?**

   A. to motivate students to do a research paper

   B. to assess prior knowledge of the students

   C. to assist in teaching skills

   D. to put events in sequential order

61. **How can the teacher establish a positive climate in the classroom?**

    A. help students see the unique contributions of individual differences

    B. use whole group instruction for all content areas

    C. help students divide into cooperative groups based on ability

    D. eliminate teaching strategies that allow students to make choices

62. **How can video laser disks be used in instruction?**

    A. students can use the laser disk to create pictures for reports

    B. students can use the laser disk to create a science experiment

    C. students can use the laser disk to record class activities

    D. students can use the laser disk to review concepts studied

63. **How can students use a computer desk-top publishing center?**

    A. to set up a classroom budget

    B. to create student made books

    C. to design a research project

    D. to create a classroom behavior management system

64. **Which of the following is an example of a synthesis question according to Bloom's taxonomy?**

    A. "What is the definition of_____?"

    B. "Compare ____ to ____."

    C. "Match column a to column B."

    D. "Propose an alternative to_____."

65. **What is a good strategy for teaching ethnically diverse students?**

    A. don't focus on the students' culture

    B. expect them to assimilate easily into your classroom

    C. imitate their speech patterns

    D. include ethnic studies into the curriculum

66. **What is a typical reason for school phobia to arise?**

    A. the child has been a scapegoat in school

    B. the teacher is rigid, punitive and overly demanding

    C. the child is developmentally not ready

    D. the child has difficulty separating from the parents

67. **On intelligence quotient scales, what is the average intelligence score?**

    A. 100 - 120

    B. 60 - 80

    C. 90 - 110

    D. 80 - 100

68. **How many stages of intellectual development does Piaget define?**

    A. two

    B. four

    C. six

    D. eight

69. **What is the most significant development emerging in children at age two?**

    A. immune system development

    B. socialization occurs

    C. language development

    D. perceptual development

70. **What is the adolescent stage of Erikson's developmental stages?**

    A. conservation vs. operation

    B. initiative vs. guilt

    C. socialization vs. intimacy

    D. identity vs. role confusion

71. **According to Piaget, when does the development of symbolic functioning and language take place?**

    A. concrete operations stage

    B. formal operations stage

    C. sensorimotor stage

    D. preoperational stage

72. **What would the presence of a low attention span and restlessness in a child be a possible indication of?**

    A. anger

    B. retardation

    C. hyperkinesis

    D. adaptation

73. **According to Haim Ginott, what do children fear the most?**

   A. hunger

   B. abandonment and loss of love

   C. shameful situations

   D. physical abuse

74. **What would be espoused by Jerome Bruner?**

   A. thought depends on the acquisition of operations

   B. memory plays a significant role in cognitive growth

   C. genetics is the most important factor for cognitive growth

   D. enriched environments have significant effects on cognitive growth

75. **What is the learning theorist's view of language acquisition?**

   A. language is shaped by the reinforcement children receive from their caretakers

   B. language is the result of innate biological mechanisms

   C. language results spontaneously

   D. language is developed through systematic instruction

76. **Why is Kohlberg's theory important to classroom teachers?**

   A. it is a theory that explains how language is acquired

   B. it is a theory that explains how complex and logical thought is developed

   C. it is a theory that explains the stages of moral development in a child

   D. it is a theory that explains the psychosocial development of the child

77. **What must be a consideration when a parent complains that he/she can't control their child's behavior?**

   A. consider whether the parent gives feedback to the child

   B. consider whether the parent's expectations for control are developmentally appropriate

   C. consider how much time the parent spends with the child

   D. consider how rigid the rules are that the parent sets

78. **Bobby, a nine year-old, has been caught stealing frequently in the classroom. What might be a factor contributing to this behavior?**

   A. need for the items stolen

   B. serious emotional disturbance

   C. desire to experiment

   D. a normal stage of development

79. **What is an event that increases the likelihood that the response it follows will occur again?**

   A. stimulus

   B. unconditioned stimulus

   C. retrieval cue

   D. reinforcer

80. **How can mnemonic devices be used to increase achievement?**

   A. they help the child rehearse the information

   B. they help the child visually imagine the information

   C. they help the child to code information

   D. they help the child reinforce concepts

81. **Which is true of child protective services?**

   A. they have been forced to become more punitive in their attempts to treat and prevent child abuse and neglect

   B. they have become more a means for identifying cases of abuse and less an agent for rehabilitation due to the large volume of cases

   C. they have become advocates for structured discipline within the school

   D. they have become a strong advocate in the court system

82. **Primarily why are operant techniques used in the classroom?**

   A. to establishment punishments

   B. to modify behaviors

   C. to change behaviors

   D. to establish behaviors

83. **What does the validity of a test refer to?**

   A. its consistency

   B. its usefulness

   C. its accuracy

   D. the degree of true scores it provides

84. **What is the best definition for an achievement test?**

   A. it measures mechanical and practical abilities

   B. it measures broad areas of knowledge that are the result of cumulative learning experiences

   C. it measures the ability to learn to perform a task

   D. it measures performance related to specific, recently-acquired information

85. In a survey of child abuse done by Gil involving 12,000 cases, what was the significant find?

    A. 75% of the abuse was inflicted by a foster sibling

    B. 86% of the abuse was inflicted by a parent or parents

    C. 95% of the cases were unfounded

    D. 25% of the cases involved sexual abuse

86. Which of the following is an accurate description of ESL students?

    A. remedial students

    B. exceptional education students

    C. are not a homogeneous group

    D. feel confident in communicating in English when with their peers

87. What is an effective way to help a non-English speaking student succeed in class?

    A. refer the child to a specialist

    B. maintain an encouraging, success-oriented atmosphere

    C. help them assimilate by making them use English exclusively

    D. help them cope with the content materials you presently use

88. What are the steps of CALLA (Cognitive Academic Language Learning Approach)?

    A. purpose, content, materials, plans

    B. description, sequence, choice, classification, principles, evaluation

    C. sentence structure, content, appearance, organization

    D. preparation, presentation, practice, evaluation, follow-up

89. What should be considered when evaluating textbooks for content?

    A. type of print used

    B. number of photos used

    C. free of cultural stereotyping

    D. outlines at the beginning of each chapter

90. How can text be modified for low level ESL students?

    A. add visuals and illustrations

    B. let students write definitions

    C. change text to a narrative form

    D. have students write details out from the text

91. **What is a feature of using the cloze procedure?**

    A. it reflects student learning with regard to curriculum objectives

    B. it provides a highly structured environment for oral speech

    C. it can be used to measure reading comprehension and achievement

    D. it encourages language production

92. **Which of the following is considered a study skill?**

    A. using graphs, tables, charts

    B. using a desk-top publishing program

    C. explaining important vocabulary words

    D. asking for clarification

93. **When using a kinesthetic approach, what would be an appropriate activity?**

    A. list

    B. match

    C. define

    D. debate

94. **Etienne is an ESL student. He has begun to engage in conversation and produce connected narrative. What developmental stage for second language acquisition is he in?**

    A. early production

    B. speech emergence

    C. preproduction

    D. intermediate fluency

95. **What is a roadblock to second language learning?**

    A. students are forced to speak

    B. student speak only when ready

    C. mistakes are considered a part of learning

    D. the focus is on oral communication

96. **What do cooperative learning methods all have in common?**

    A. philosophy

    B. cooperative task/cooperative reward structures

    C. student roles and communication

    D. teacher roles

97. **Who developed the theory of multiple intelligences?**

   A. Bruner

   B. Gardner

   C. Kagan

   D. Cooper

98. **What did Johnston and Allington discover in their study of "pull-out" programs?**

   A. they are effective for low SES students

   B. children typically only need one or two years in the program to reach grade level

   C. no substantial improvement was shown in reading

   D. the regular education program is improved

99. **What did Gamoran discover in the study on tracking children?**

   A. the children in the bottom track achieved less that similar children placed in an untracked class

   B. the children in the bottom track achieved more that similar children placed in an untracked class

   C. no significant data was found

   D. the best teacher was assigned to the low track

100. **When is content teaching effective?**

   A. when it is presented in demonstration form

   B. when the teacher separates the content into distinct elements

   C. when the content is covered over a long span of time

   D. when the decision about content is made at the district level

101. **According to recent studies, what is the estimated number of adolescents that have physical, social, or emotional problems related to the abuse of alcohol?**

   A. less that one million

   B. 1-2 million

   C. 2-3 million

   D. over four million

102. **The teacher states, "We will work on the first page of vocabulary words. On the second page we will work on the structure and meaning of the words. We will go over these together and then you will write out the answers to the exercises on your own. I will be circulating to give help if needed". What is this an example of?**

   A. evaluation of instructional activity

   B. analysis of instructional activity

   C. identification of expected outcomes

   D. pacing of instructional activity

103. **If teachers attend to content, instructional materials, activities, learner needs, and goals in instructional planning, what could be an outcome?**

A. ease in planning for the next school year

B. effective classroom performance

C. elevated test scores on standardized tests

D. more student involvement

104. **According to research, what can be a result of specific teacher actions on behavior?**

A. increase in student misconduct

B. increase in the number of referrals

C. decrease in student participation

D. decrease in student retentions

105. **What is the definition of proactive classroom management?**

A. management that is constantly changing

B. management that is downplayed

C. management that gives clear and explicit instructions and rewards compliance

D. management that is designed by the students

106. **In Kounin's study of desist techniques, which desist had a consistent effect?**

A. clarity of desist

B. roughness of desist

C. task-focus desist

D. approval-focus desist

107. **Why is it important for the teacher to alert non-performers when conducting activities?**

A. it creates suspense

B. students will take over the discipline

C. students will become more work involved

D. students will more likely not take part in the recitation

108. **What might be a result if the teacher is distracted by some unrelated event in the instruction?**

A. students will leave the class

B. students will understand the importance of class rules

C. students will stay on-task longer

D. students will lose the momentum of the lesson

109. **Why is praise for compliance important in classroom management?**

    A. students will continue deviant behavior

    B. desirable conduct will be repeated

    C. it reflects simplicity and warmth

    D. students will fulfill obligations

110. **What is an effective amount of "wait time"?**

    A. one second

    B. 5 seconds

    C. 15 seconds

    D. 10 seconds

111. **Mr. Perez has the pictures and maps ready for his lesson. The movie is set up to go, and he tested the operation of the machine before the class came in. What is this an example of?**

    A. controlled interruptions

    B. housekeeping

    C. punctuality

    D. management transition

112. **Mrs. Shapiro states, "During the past four weeks we have discussed national and international conditions which led to the outbreak of World War II. Tomorrow we are going to spend some time going over them again and comparing and contrasting them with conditions in the world today. Make a list of these conditions from your class notes, and let's see how complete our lists are". What is this an example of?**

    A. topic summary within the lesson

    B. weekly summary and recap

    C. lesson-end review

    D. test preparation

113. **What has research shown to be the effect of using advance organizers in the lesson?**

    A. they facilitate learning and retention

    B. they enhance retention only

    C. they only serve to help the teacher organize the lesson

    D. they show definitive positive results on student achievement

114. **How are standardized tests useful in assessment?**

    A. for teacher evaluation

    B. for evaluation of the administration

    C. for comparison from school to school

    D. for comparison to the population on which the test was normed

115. **Ms. Smith says, "Yes, exactly what do you mean by 'It was the author's intention to mislead you'?". What does this illustrate?**

   A. digression

   B. restates response

   C. probes a response

   D. amplifies a response

116. **What is a frequently used type of feedback to students?**

   A. correctives

   B. simple praise-confirmation

   C. correcting the response

   D. explanations

117. **What is the effect when combining homework with review?**

   A. better classroom management

   B. better instructional planning

   C. enhanced effectiveness of the test

   D. enhanced effectiveness of the homework and review

118. **Which of the following is a law-like principle?**

   A. water is an odorless, tasteless liquid

   B. the story <u>The Grapes of Wrath</u> is a great work of literature

   C. if people are persecuted for their religious beliefs, they will flee to a place where their beliefs will be tolerated

   D. a parallelogram consists of two parallel sides

119. **What can be concluded from research on concept teaching?**

   A. the most effective way is oral presentation and visual examples

   B. the most effective way is to use manipulatives and oral presentation

   C. the most effective way is to use a definition with examples and non-examples

   D. the most effective way is to use visuals and manipulation

120. **Mr. Brown states, "A parallelogram has two parallel sides. But remember, and this is important, a parallelogram with opposite sides equal is called a rhombus." What does this illustrate?**

   A. examples and non-examples

   B. repetition

   C. marker technique

   D. marker expression

121. **What is it called when a teacher uses colored marking pens to color code words with long and short vowels?**

   A. examples and non-examples

   B. repetition

   C. marker technique

   D. marker expression

122. **According to Erikson's theory of psychosocial development, what are the significant relations that the child has during the latency stage (6-12 years)?**

   A. parents

   B. family

   C. school and neighborhood

   D. leadership models

123. **What is perhaps the most controversial issue in developmental psychology?**

   A. interactionism

   B. nature vs. nature

   C. relevance of IQ scores

   D. change vs. external events

124. **What is Bruner's final stage of cognitive development?**

   A. symbolic

   B. conventional

   C. latency

   D. postconventional

125. **According to Piaget, what is a child born with?**

   A. the tendency to actively relate pieces of information acquired

   B. the ability to adapt

   C. primary emotions

   D. desire

126. **A child exhibits the following symptoms: a lack of emotional responsivity, indifference to physical contact, abnormal social play, and abnormal speech. What is the likely diagnosis for this child?**

   A. separation anxiety

   B. mental retardation

   C. autism

   D. hypochondria

127. **Research on short-term memory has suggested which of the following?**

  A. the capacity is unlimited

  B. information must be rehearsed since it fades within 30 seconds

  C. has high retrieval

  D. it processes information in depth

128. **What is the definition of a non-performer?**

  A. students who are off-task

  B. students not chosen to answer a teacher-posed question

  C. students with stanine scores of 20 or below

  D. students who consistently score below 50 percent on classroom tests

129. **What is not a way that teachers show acceptance and give value to a student response?**

  A. acknowledging

  B. correcting

  C. discussing

  D. amplifying

130. **What is teacher withitness?**

  A. having adequate knowledge of subject matter

  B. a skill that must be mastered to attain certification

  C. understanding the current fads and trends that affect students

  D. attending to two tasks at once

131. **What should the teacher do when a student is tapping a pencil on the desk during a lecture?**

  A. stop the lesson and correct the student as an example to other students

  B. walk over to the student and quietly touch the pencil as a signal for the student to stop

  C. announce to the class that everyone should remember to remain quiet during the lecture

  D. ignore the student, hoping he or she will stop

132. **The teacher responds, "Yes, that is correct" to a student's answer. What is this an example of?**

  A. academic feedback

  B. academic praise

  C. simple positive response

  D. simple negative response

133. **Which of the following is not a characteristic of effective praise?**

   A. praise is delivered in front of the class so it will serve to motivate others

   B. praise is low-key

   C. praise provides information about student competence

   D. praise is delivered contingently

134. **What is teacher redirects?**

   A. the teacher redirects the deviant behavior to another task

   B. the teacher changes the focus of the class to provide smooth transitions

   C. the teacher changes student jobs every nine weeks

   D. the teacher asks a second student to expound on the first student's answer

135. **What is a lesson-initiating review?**

   A. beginning a new lesson with a review of the previous lesson

   B. listing the key points of a lesson at the beginning of the lesson

   C. a lesson based solely on review materials

   D. reviewing key points of the lesson at the end of the lesson.

136. **Reviews during the lesson lead to which of the following?**

   A. a loss of class momentum

   B. confusion if done before the students have internalized the subject matter

   C. greater subject matter retention

   D. disjointed lessons

137. **A teacher stops the lecture to recap the important points. What is this called?**

   A. lesson-initiating review

   B. lesson-end review

   C. topic summary within the lesson review

   D. global-review

138. **Which of the following is not a specific learning outcome?**

   A. a global statement

   B. exclusive to the current lesson

   C. determines the student performances required for mastery

   D. encompassed by the instructional objective

139. **Which of the following test items is not objective?**

    A. multiple choice

    B. essay

    C. matching

    D. true/false

140. **Which of the following is not used in evaluating test items?**

    A. student feedback

    B. content validity

    C. reliability

    D. ineffective coefficient

ANSWER KEY FOR PROFESSIONAL EDUCATOR EXAM

1	C	36.	D	71.	D	106.	B
2.	B	37.	A	72.	C	107.	C
3.	D	38.	A	73.	B	108.	D
4.	A	39.	D	74.	D	109.	B
5	A	40.	C	75.	A	110.	B
6.	D	41.	B	76.	C	111.	B
7.	A	42.	B	77.	B	112.	C
8.	D	43.	B	78.	B	113.	A
9.	A	44.	B	79.	D	114.	D
10.	C	45.	C	80.	B	115.	C
11.	B	46.	C	81.	B	116.	B
12.	C	47.	C	82.	B	117.	D
13.	A	48.	B	83.	B	118.	C
14.	D	49.	B	84.	B	119.	C
15.	B	50.	C	85.	B	120.	D
16.	C	51.	C	86.	C	121.	C
17.	C	52.	B	87.	B	122.	C
18.	D	53.	D	88.	D	123.	B
19.	C	54.	A	89.	C	124.	A
20.	B	55.	B	90.	A	125.	A
21.	D	56.	B	91.	C	126.	C
22.	B	57.	C	92.	A	127.	B
23.	B	58.	B	93.	B	128.	B
24.	C	59.	C	94.	D	129.	B
25.	D	60.	B	95.	A	130.	D
26.	B	61.	A	96.	B	131.	B
27.	C	62.	D	97.	B	132.	C
28.	A	63.	B	98.	C	133.	A
29.	C	64.	D	99.	A	134.	D
30.	B	65.	D	100.	B	135.	A
31.	C	66.	D	101.	D	136.	B
32.	B	67.	C	102.	B	137.	C
33.	A	68.	B	103.	B	138.	A
34	B	69.	C	104.	A	139.	B
35.	D	70.	D	105.	C	140.	D

This guide for the Florida Teacher Certification Exam depends on two major opinion sources: professional reviewers and you, the person actually using the book. Please help us and the users of the next edition by returning this survey to A.S.A.P. ABSTRACTS PUBLISHING 1710 Tiffany Drive
West Palm Beach, FL 33407. Or call 1-407-845-6899. Customer Service number 407-738-5445.

1. Can you offer any suggestions for improving the quality of this preview ?

2. Are there any questions that were unclear?

3. Are there any questions that you liked the most?

4. Are there any questions that you thought should have been covered but were not?

5. Any closing comments you care to make would be appreciated.

6. Would you let us use your name as a contributing editor?

Thank you for your help. Please take 10% off your next order as our way of saying thank you for filling in this survey.